Architecture
Without Rules

Architecture Without Rules

The Houses of
Marcel Breuer and
Herbert Beckhard

By David Masello

W.W. Norton & Company
New York London

To my parents, Sonia and Thomas,
who always encouraged my love of
cities and buildings, from taking
me on regular trips to Chicago's
Loop and drives through the North
Shore suburbs to supplying me
with countless pieces of Lego and
allowing me to spend entire
Saturdays and Sundays by myself
going up and down Evanston's
Grosse Pointe Lighthouse.

Text and display of this book set
in Trade Gothic
Book design by Katy Homans
and Philip Kovacevich

First published as a Norton paperback 1996

Library of Congress
Cataloging-in-Publication-Data

Masello, David
Architecture Without Rules : The houses of
Marcel Breuer and Herbert Beckhard / by
David Masello.
p. cm
1. Breuer, Marcel, 1902- --Criticism and
interpretation. 2. Beckhard, Herbert--Criticism
and interpretation. 3. Architect-designed
houses--United States. 4. Architecture,
Modern--20th century--United States. I. Title
NA 737.B68M37 1993
728' .37'0922--dc20
92-32187

ISBN 0-393-31375-1

W. W. Norton & Company, Inc.
500 Fifth Avenue, New York, N.Y. 10110
www.wwnorton.com

W. W. Norton & Company Ltd.
Castle House, 75/76 Wells Street, London W1T 3QT

3 4 5 6 7 8 9 0

Table of Contents

Architecture
Without Rules

The city is a place where a small
boy, as he walks through it, may
see something that will tell him
what he wants to do his whole life.
—Louis Kahn

Marcel Breuer (right)
and Herbert Beckhard
on a trip to Japan,
circa 1971
photo: Yoshinibu Ashihara

Introduction

In recalling a painting he once did as a teenager of a bleak, burned-out swamp area, Herbert Beckhard says that he was able to see "color in the black" and articulate that vision on the canvas. Marcel Breuer (1902–1981) said in a lecture he delivered in 1931 at the Technical University in Delft that "I consider 'white' a very versatile and beautiful color; at the same time it is the brightest color—there is seldom a reason to replace it with any other color." It would not be until 1952 that Breuer and Beckhard would begin an historic collaboration as architects, but clearly there was an earlier common link between them.

As a basic dynamic, their buildings, and especially the approximately thirty houses they designed together over a twenty-eight-year affiliation, embody ideals of distillation—that even if black and white were all that existed, Breuer and Beckhard could create from them an infinite and appealing variety of colors. Their buildings are comprised of a highly eclectic, limited palette of materials, colors, and forms combined in such a way, though, that every structure is its own composition. Despite similarities among the houses, such as fieldstone walls, uninterrupted glazed surfaces, floating and earthbound forms, and open plans, each house reflects the architects' ability to be creative and resourceful, as well as to meet the very real needs of the client. Breuer warned, in fact, that architecture's "objective is general

usefulness, including its visual impact," and a house should never be "a mere self-portrait of the architect or the client, though it must contain personal elements of both." Later he added that "architecture is where structure, function, and abstract or pure form are developed to the same degree. When one is developed at the expense of the other, there is a decadence or carelessness that I call vanity."

Despite the many important large buildings for which Marcel Breuer is immediately cited—the Whitney Museum, the UNESCO headquarters, St. John's Abbey Church, the Research Center for IBM, the Housing and Urban Development Headquarters—he is best known as an innovative master designer on a small scale. Certainly his furniture designs, particularly the nearly ubiquitous "Breuer" or "Cesca" chair (named for his daughter), and the "Wassily" chair (named for his Bauhaus cohort, the artist Wassily Kandinsky), point to his mastery on a diminutive scale; but his houses are perhaps even fuller expressions. Houses require architects, in a way that larger projects with their more complex client teams cannot, to be unwaveringly attentive to every surface and detail. In 1966, already long recognized as one of architecture's most established practitioners and the winner along with Beckhard of numerous awards, Breuer remarked in an interview with *Architectural Record* that his firm

still took the time to design one or two private houses a year because such "work represents, in a way, a laboratory department of our office. We can develop ideas and details for a client, on a relatively small scale, which we could not develop in a larger project." Virtually all of the Breuer and Beckhard houses have received awards—from the American Institute of Architects and from professional periodicals like *Architectural Record*, which has named most of their houses "Record Houses," a much-coveted industry distinction.

Breuer's design for his first wholly new house, the Harnismacher house, erected in Wiesbaden, Germany, in 1932 when he was thirty, already reveals a preoccupation with experimentation and the application of all that he learned as a furniture designer and interior designer to a free-standing structure. Breuer had never received any formal training as an architect—and never would—and so his response to this project and all others was instinctive, not unlike Frank Lloyd Wright or Thomas Jefferson.

Situated in a suburban neighborhood of imposing late-nineteenth-century houses, with their turrets, quirky towering roof forms punctured by multiple chimneys, eyebrow windows, and intricate applied sculpted elements, Breuer's restrained, horizontally emphasized house was startling. Unlike the other houses, which were as extravagantly detailed on

The Whitney
Museum, New York,
New York, 1966.
Marcel Breuer with
Hamilton Smith
photo: Ezra Stoller © Esto

their front facades as on the rear and so seemed indifferent to the various dynamics of their sites, Breuer's remained private from the road side by having few windows. But on the garden side, facing south, the house was marked by fully fenestrated walls rimmed with gleaming metal frames that took advantage of the sun and the attractive site. While neighboring houses were decidedly masonry, the Harnismacher was essentially a steel frame and concrete structure to which an off-white stucco was applied. Reinforced concrete staircases with daringly minimal railings led down to the hilly site from two terraces. Vigorously articulated and juxtaposed

fieldstone walls were erected on the site. White was used for all interior surfaces, and much of the furniture was black. It was in the house's contrasts—monochromatic walls and furniture against colored rugs and objects, solid walls and glazed ones, natural materials like fieldstone and those like reinforced concrete that revealed human intervention, and the idea that interior spaces can be extended to exterior spaces— that a great harmony was created.

Beckhard's work, too, exemplifies the ability to be an especially innovative and expert designer on a small scale. In a highly productive and varied career as an employee, then an associate and finally a partner with Breuer and continuing now with his own Manhattan-based firm, Herbert Beckhard Frank Richlan & Associates, Beckhard has designed a significant number of buildings, ranging from churches, schools, and industrial buildings to college facilities and office structures. It is his houses, though, that best sum up his architectural agenda and concerns.

Despite a constantly growing and active practice involving large building commissions, Breuer and Beckhard were intent always on securing house commissions. As head of his own firm today, which is a direct descendant of the firm founded by Marcel Breuer, Beckhard continues to secure house projects, even though the majority of his work comes from major corporations, public and

educational institutions, and foreign and domestic governments. Clearly, designing houses cannot approximate the financial rewards of large-scale commercial projects and they always require just as much work. But nothing can compare with the intimacy that goes into designing a house and the freedom of expression that each commission allows.

Beckhard and Breuer almost always established a genuine friendship with the client. In discussing the program for a house, clients have to tell architects remarkably intimate details about their lives, and architects have to ask equally intimate questions to devise a plan that makes sense: are children planned, will meals be eaten together or separately, are there any physical disabilities that need to be accounted for, will there be much entertaining, are there art collections to be displayed? Given such issues, there is nothing routine about designing a house; and for serious architects like Breuer and Beckhard, that chance for limitless creativity is alluring. Also, an unusual number of their clients have been serious art collectors, and clearly these people see the houses they commission as the ultimate expression of their aesthetic concerns.

Fundamentally, a house that an architect designs influences the lives of its occupants. Given that kind of responsibility, Breuer and Beckhard have long recognized that an active client, one who acts

University of
Massachusetts
Campus Center,
Amherst, Mas-
sachusetts, 1969.
Marcel Breuer and
Herbert Beckhard

St. Francis de Sales
Church, Muskegon,
Michigan, 1964.
Marcel Breuer and
Herbert Beckhard

as a true collaborator and not as
an obstructor, is a favored one.
Clients who participate in the process drive architects on to further
solutions.

History has demonstrated that
Modern architecture of substance
has fared well in the architectural
spectrum. Though challenged by
Postmodernism, Modern design
has showed a certain logic and
resilience and an ability to per-
severe amid assorted stylistic
movements (Deconstructivism
being merely the latest casualty).
    It was because of one of
Modern architecture's greatest
attributes that it was criticized.
Modern buildings are economical
to build. They are void of extraneous costly detail; they incorporate state-of-the-art construction
techniques; and they can be con-
structed relatively quickly. As a
result, such precepts were exploited and misused. Inferior
Modern-style buildings appeared
in great numbers and came to
define entire city skylines in the
late 1950s through the 1970s. In
their worst incarnations, Modern
urban buildings were indifferent to
the street, pedestrians, and landscape; so for many people Post-
modern buildings with their deliberate references to the past, playful geometries, ornament, and
surface detailing were welcome.
In their best articulations, however, Modern buildings transformed the urban agenda and
landscape. Despite such variables,
Breuer and Beckhard's visions,

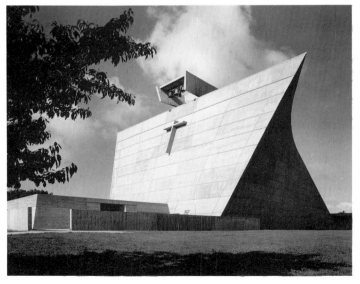

Partial view of
the east facade of
the Housing and
Urban Development
Headquarters Build-
ing, Washington,
D.C., 1968. Marcel
Breuer and Herbert
Beckhard, with
Nolen-Swinburne
and Associates
photo: Ben Schnall

The Museum of
Modern Art Exhi-
bition House, New
York, New York,
1949. Marcel Breuer
photo: Ezra Stoller © Esto

whether for houses or commercial buildings, remained consistent and pure. They pursued form, space, and function as governing principles of every design.

American suburbs have been marked for decades by period styles—Tudor, Gothic, and Colonial among them. Even during the explosive growth of suburbia following World War II, traditional vernacular forms remained in force and were favored by buyers. After all, few were familiar with Modern buildings and when different houses like those of Breuer's and Beckhard's appeared on such historicist, bucolic streets, many residents thought they were blasphemous. Where were the shutters, porches, meandering pathways, mullions, pitched roof forms, small punched windows, shingles, brickwork, and all the

other design features for which suburban homes were known? Like many of the great Modern sky-scrapers—Lever House, the Seagram building, the former PepsiCo headquarters—Breuer and Beckhard houses have en-dured because they are original visions embodying an uncompro-mising integrity of design.

Modern architects have some-times been defined as those who ignore past building design princi-ples—period styles, ornament, traditional detailing, playful and whimsical interpretations of the building envelope—in favor of pure, austere design requisites. Yet, the irony is that those archi-tects who refuse to indulge in pale or literal imitations of buildings from a past age and past technol-ogy perhaps most respect old buildings and heed the important

lessons inherent in them. For architects like Breuer and Beckhard, great old buildings are just that—built entities appropri-ate for certain times, technology, clients, functions, and societal needs. For Beckhard, the notion of copying, alluding to, or recreating features of old buildings makes no sense. Why create an inferior version? Decades ago Modernists believed that a new vision was needed. Why build a house or skyscraper that mimics the past but isn't really of it? Not only can it never be of the past but by nature of it having enough of the past about it, it can never really be a part of the future either.

In examining architecture of the past, Beckhard honed in on specific dynamics that were apart from the ornament and detail: is the space well defined and func-

"Cesca" chair,
1928.
photo: Collection, The
Museum of Modern Art,
New York

"Wassily" chair,
1927–28.
photo: Collection, The
Museum of Modern Art,
New York

tional, how is it lit, what is its form, what materials are used, what is the spatial effect, what lessons does the building hold for today's buildings?

Beckhard has stated that one of his main objections to contemporary trends in architecture is the willful indifference to technology. While today's consumer watches large-screen high-resolution television, drives state-of-the-art cars, listens to compact discs, and flies in airplanes that cross continents in a few hours, some architects build buildings that seek to deny such an evolution. A case in point is the window. Modern architects embraced the development that allows for large-scale uninterrupted glazed walls. Glass no longer (for decades at this point) has to be subdivided by panes and mullions. Windows can be vast and can be opened fully, allowing for a maximum interplay between outside and inside space.

In terms of structure, Modern houses like those by Breuer and Beckhard prove that large open interior spaces can be spanned with greater structural efficiency than ever before, resulting in Breuer's admitted goal of more space with less mass. Old houses needed many supporting walls which meant smaller rooms. In Modern houses, whole walls can be eliminated, opening up space in ways never before imagined and still allowing for privacy and definition of room function. Breuer stated, in essence, in the Reed & Barton Design Lecture he delivered

at the University of Michigan in 1963, that the great structures of the past—the Egyptian pyramids, the Parthenon, the Eiffel Tower, the Brooklyn Bridge, the Gothic arch, the Renaissance dome, the Mayan temple—are those that embrace the technology of their time to the fullest. The "clearly visible working of the material . . . is an 'architectural' expression," he said. Taking an extreme stance, Beckhard has remarked that he would prefer that the term "Modern architecture" be dropped and replaced with "Logical architecture" for that is what he feels his buildings are most about.

While Breuer and Beckhard houses are highly individual entities, they can be grouped roughly, in terms of plan, into two basic types: "long" houses in which living areas

are situated at one end, kitchen and other service utilities in the center, and bedrooms at the far end; and "bi-nuclear" houses, a term Breuer invented but rarely if ever used, in which sleeping and living activities are more emphatically separate from each other, often to the point where children's bedrooms might be situated in a wing wholly separate from that reserved for adults. And though an open plan prevails in their houses, there is little chance of ambiguity for each activity zone is clearly articulated. A children's/family room may be at the center of a wing of a house but it never gets confused with another living space; and while living and dining areas often meld there is a distinct sense of where each room's appropriate activity is to take place. There is no rigidity in function.

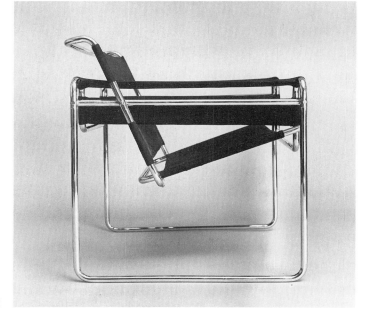

Gane Pavilion,
Bristol, England,
1936. Marcel Breuer
photo: Collection, The
Museum of Modern Art,
New York

Frank House,
Pittsburgh,
Pennsylvania,
1939. Marcel
Breuer with
Walter Gropius
photo: Ezra Stoller © Esto

The usefulness of the house is stressed. While some architects might wish clients to consult with them every time they want to buy a new ashtray to make sure it does not compromise the aesthetic purity, Breuer and Beckhard are able to step away from a project once it is done and let the occupants live in it as they wish. "I welcome art as an addition to the architecture, the same way that I welcome people, flowers, books—signs of living and usage for which the space is the container," Breuer once said.

Though Breuer had been building houses for more than a decade that embodied these plan dynamics, it was not until 1949 that his ideas were presented to the public, and in such a way that the public could actually occupy such spaces, albeit for short amounts of time. The Museum of Modern Art in New York commissioned Breuer to construct a single-family house in its sculpture garden. The complete, freestanding suburban house, occupying nearly the entire garden of the museum, had as its backdrop the towers of Rockefeller Center and a row of nineteenth-century limestone townhouses. The house was meant to be a practical solution for a suburban family where the breadwinner, the man, commutes to the city every day, returning in the evening to his wife and two children. The rectangular house had two bedrooms at one end, one for the children and a larger one for the adults, as well as a cen-

trally located playroom. Yet, as the result of an upward-sloping butterfly roof, the other end of the house became two stories, the ground floor for the garage and the second floor for the master bedroom and bath; in so doing, a separate wing of the house was created. Depending on a family's need for privacy or on whether children are still living with their parents, the house can be both "bi-nuclear" and "long." Children can have their own apartment of sorts complete with bedroom and playroom, while the adults have their private wing, or the family can be grouped together. Inexpensive to build, adaptable, practical, with interesting living spaces, and an elegant form, "The House in the Museum Garden," as it was known, revealed a real solution for a kind of housing that America was coming to need and embrace on a massive scale.

Breuer and Beckhard houses not only exemplify, but have often determined, the ideals of Modern residential architecture. Their houses often downplay their fronts or entrance facades—largely because of privacy concerns but also as a way to heighten the sense of discovery or adventure about a house. Entrances, such as at the Robeck house or the Cohen house, are often slightly hidden so that visitors and the occupants are enticed to investigate the space. At the Stillman II house, for instance, an entrance stairway encased by fieldstone walls makes the visitor aware of the material's texture and

**Marcel Breuer's
Lincoln, Massachusetts,
House, 1939**
photo: Ezra Stoller © Esto

hues. At some houses, such as the Breuer/Bratti house and the Schwartz house, garages and driveways are positioned well away from the entrance door so that there is a chance to decompress from the automobile. Rather than simply driving up to a house or into a garage and immediately entering a door, visitors are made to approach the house from a distance that allows them, and indeed forces them, to think about the form they are about to enter. Driveways themselves can be deliberately casual and curvaceous as a way to prolong the arrival.

Another strongly articulated dynamic is the play between transparent and solid. Elevations of houses are usually either wholly glazed or solid, and rarely do the treatments ever turn a corner. Often, a solid plane (perhaps a fieldstone wall) will extend beyond the edge of a house into the landscape. These fin walls enlarge the envelope of the house and capture additional space.

The melding of interior with exterior living spaces is endemic to Breuer and Beckhard houses. Glazed walls can have the sense of extending the boundaries of a room. Courtyards, terraces defined by low-rising fieldstone walls, pronounced entrance overhangs, and open roof forms foster this sense of capturing additional space. Often, materials used on exteriors translate to interiors, further confusing the boundaries between outdoors and indoors. In some cases, such as in Breuer's

own house in Lincoln, Massachusetts, and Beckhard's own home in Glen Cove, New York, massive fireplaces are inserted in fieldstone walls that act as room dividers. In Breuer's Chamberlain Cottage or Beckhard's Rosenberg house, the fireplaces become freestanding sculptural objects. In other houses by the architects, fireplaces can be simple boxes of white painted brick or more sensuous bush-hammered concrete forms. Fieldstone walls that frame a courtyard, such as at the Stillman II house, can reappear inside as a continuous window seat/display ledge.

There is a rigorous denial of extraneous detail on Breuer and Beckhard houses, though innovative and practical applications of state-of-the-art technology can wind up becoming decorative elements. At the Starkey house, the solar control devices, while highly practical, are also appealing

and relatively complex elements, and the impact of the house would be considerably lessened without them.

Solar devices are but one indication of the architects' conspicuous articulation of structure. Beams from which roofs are hung, such as at the Starkey house, are laminated not only for protection from the elements but as a way to draw attention to them. Narrow steel pins emerge from wood posts over which houses are cantilevered, such as at the McMullen beach house. A large truss is brought inside the porch at the Wise house and becomes an important interior detail. "This achievement of expression is art," Breuer said in the Reed & Barton Design Lecture.

Many of the architects' houses "float" above their sites by means of posts, trusses, and supporting walls. This gravity-defying notion—Breuer called it an

Geller House,
Lawrence, Long Is-
land, New York, 1945.
Marcel Breuer
photo: Ezra Stoller © Esto

Chamberlain Cot-
tage, Wayland,
Massachusetts,
1940. Marcel Breuer
with Walter Gropius
photo: Ezra Stoller © Esto

"atavistic instinct"—accomplishes several things. The landscape remains undisturbed, additional exterior living spaces result, views can be maximized, privacy is retained, and a house's inherent structure can be fully revealed. In the Wise house, these dynamics are taken to their extreme, for the landscape literally flows beneath the house and out the other side. The undulating terrain and the way it changes becomes an integral part of the facades of the house. By nature of being elevated, these houses must be light and so most are made of cypress or cedar wood. Houses made of stone, however, are earthbound, sculptural presences. The Hooper house is among the most dramatic examples of the stone houses. The house takes as its form a single, uninterrupted, horizontal line with a broad glazed entryway cut into it. One of the reasons it is thought Breuer decided to build a second house

for himself and his family in New Canaan, Connecticut, was that the second site, more level than the first, allowed him to build a house out of stone, a material he was eager to experiment with and exploit.

It is no coincidence that many Breuer and Beckhard houses are on sloping sites. It is not easy to accommodate a traditional style house on hilly land; Colonial, Tudor, typical suburban ranches, have set design agendas. They need to perch on flat sites, with all elevations fully revealed. Because Modern houses can take whatever form they want, virtually no site is unbuildable. Beckhard's Cohen house is situated on a site in one of the most desirable neighbor-hoods in South Orange, New Jersey, filled with decades-old traditional style houses. But be-cause the plot of land was narrow, shady, and marked by steep hill-sides it was thought to be unusable.

As a result of the hillsides, many of the houses incorporate earthbound and gravity-defying elements. The garage elements of both the Starkey house in Duluth, Minnesota, and the Reed house in Danbury, Connecticut, are stone structures that are anchored to the earth, while just beyond, the houses cantilever over their sites, defying the land and also taking the best advantage of it. At the Gagarin house in Litchfield, Connecticut, one arrives at what appears to be a rather modest one-story house. Once inside, however,

it becomes evident that the house is burrowed into a hillside and that there is another expansive story below.

The facile characterization that Modern buildings by defin-ition are machines made for living—with strict linear expres-sions, man-made materials or natural ones fashioned in such a way that all natural features are obliterated, and a rigorous balance in the composition—is an erron-eous one for Breuer and Beckhard houses. Modern buildings are often regarded as being indifferent to context, built and natural, but Breuer and Beckhard houses are contextual. Whenever possible, local, indigenous materials are used. The Hooper house in Baltimore uses Maryland field-stone; the Koerfer house in Switzerland uses local quarried stone and stucco, the latter a common building material in that country; and the Bornhorst house has panels of local Vermont stone. Consequently, the architects' houses often embrace vernacular traditions. Even natural elements such as trees, old stone walls, and topographical features are often retained.

Concomitant with this bow to local building traditions and forms—a denial of the Modernist machine in favor of a more human entity—is the deliberate asymme-try that characterizes the houses. Doorways are often not centered in the front elevation, windows are never perfect squares, fin walls skew the precise lines of a house,

and cutouts in roofs and in court-yard walls are off-center. Also, garden walls, retaining walls, and driveways are free-flowing forms that are foils to the otherwise linear emphasis of the houses. But the most important indication that the houses are oriented for humans and not machines is their unpredictability. Every house is different and every elevation on every house is varied.

Marcel Lajos Breuer was born in Pecs, Hungary, in 1902. At eighteen, after a brief and impatient period at Vienna's Academy of Art, he enrolled as a student in Walter Gropius's newly founded Bauhaus in Weimar. Breuer had left the Academy of Art because he found the program too theoretical and he craved a much more practical agenda. The carpentry or woodworking workshop at the Bauhaus seemed the ideal arena for a hands-on experience.

Breuer spent four years at the Bauhaus where he distinguished himself with several notable furniture designs, including a series of pieces for an experimental house that was shown at the Bauhaus exhibition in 1922. After Breuer's graduation in 1924, political pressures forced the closure of the Bauhaus school and Breuer went to live and work in Paris.

Gropius resurrected the school in Dessau, Germany, in 1925 and Breuer returned as Master of the woodworking shop. Eager to foster ties with industry and manufacturers, Gropius emphasized that the Bauhaus was not craft-oriented, but was instead geared to creating designs that could be easily mass-produced and thus have mass appeal. Within only three months at the new institution, Breuer, inspired so the legend goes by the handlebars of his new Adler bicycle, designed the first of his tubular steel chairs, for which his name would eventually become synonymous. The Club Chair Model B3 became known as the "Wassily" chair when the artist Wassily Kandinsky decided to use it for his staff house on the Bauhaus campus. Soon a major furniture manufacturer, Thonet, agreed to mass-produce the chair for residential use, the first time a metal chair had ever been considered for use in a place other than an office.

By 1928, after having left the Bauhaus to begin an architectural practice in Berlin, Breuer designed his even more famous chair, the

"Cesca" chair, a cantilevered composition with a continuous tubular steel frame, cane seat, and black bentwood back. Also known as the eponymous Breuer chair, it remains among the most common pieces of furniture in houses, offices, and schools worldwide. Breuer's comments on it also reflect his feelings about how he built his houses: "The most up-to-date material—chrome steel—contrasts with the oldest material—cane seating and wood. I have never had the feeling that certain materials were acceptable and others were not. . . . What I always aimed for was freedom in exploring materials, new and old, and freedom in exploring technological disciplines."

While in Berlin Breuer secured notable interior design commissions and two architectural commissions—the Harnismacher house in 1932 and the Doldertal Apartments, designed with Alfred and Emil Roth, in Zurich in 1935. While both of these projects reflected Breuer's interest in light, floating, elevated forms, his Gane Pavilion, which was erected for the Royal Agricultural Show in Bristol in 1936, showed a new concern with mass.

Because of increasing political unrest in Germany and Hitler's opposition to Modern art, Breuer relocated to England in 1935 and formed a partnership with F. R. S. Yorke. His first commission was for the renovation of the house of Grofton Gane, a manufacturer and distributor of

Perry House, New
Milford, Connecticut,
1952. Herbert
Beckhard with
William Landsberg,
Associate Architect
photo: Joseph W. Molitor

Modern furniture. The exhibition
pavilion was meant to be an ideal
forum for displaying some of the
original and reproduction pieces
that Gane's company, P. E. Gane
Ltd., was producing. Though the
open-plan structure was meant to
represent a house it did not need
to contain a kitchen or bathroom.
Some of the central dynamics that
would characterize Breuer houses
for the rest of his career were
spawned with this commission.
Exterior and some interior walls
comprised of local Cotswold stone
were juxtaposed with full-height
glass walls, some of which were
sliding doors. His use of local
stone showed that Modern buildings could accommodate vernacular forms and materials very
well. Cutout roof forms and cross
beams captured, or at least suggested, additional exterior living
spaces.

Long in contact and asso-
ciation with Gropius since the

Bauhaus days, Breuer left England
in 1937 for Cambridge where
Gropius, who had emigrated previously, had secured a teaching job
for Breuer at Harvard. The two
immediately began a collaboration
on a number of American houses.
Among the first was the Frank
house in Pittsburgh, a large four-
story "International Style" residence with client requirements
that included six bedrooms, nine
bathrooms, an indoor heated
swimming pool, and several other
spaces such as receiving halls,
bars, and sitting rooms. Though
busier in form and material than
any other Breuer house—largely
because the client kept wanting to
make the house bigger and show-
ier—trademark Breuer details
emerge: pronounced overhangs
over entryways, the use of local
fieldstone, a massive fieldstone
fireplace, and cantilevered
elements.

In a small house Breuer built
for himself in Lincoln, Massachusetts, in 1939 (he also collaborated with Gropius on his house in
the same town), he fashioned a
two-level residence, open in plan,
that featured three levels of living
area. What is essentially a wooden
rectangular box contains two bedrooms, two baths, a kitchen, a
maid's room, and a dining room.
The living room is situated in
between the other two levels in a
split-level configuration, and so its
ceiling is especially high. The
living area features full-height
glass walls juxtaposed with a solid
fieldstone wall, in which is cut a

simple fireplace opening.

For Henry G. Chamberlain, a
professor at Harvard, Breuer and
Gropius built in 1940 a small
weekend house in Wayland,
Massachusetts, that received
considerable attention. The house,
sheathed in unpainted vertical
cypress boarding, cantilevered
dramatically over a stone base; its
interior living area focused on a
stone fireplace with a notch taken
out from one corner and a tiny
rectangular pass-through element.
The fireplace acts as both a room
divider and a sculptural piece, one
of the first times that Breuer made
the fireplace a freestanding object.
In Breuer's 1945 Tompkins house
in Hewlett Harbor, Long Island,
the freestanding fireplace features
a hearth open on both sides of the
wall. One wall of windows, comprised of clear and opaque panes,
emphasizes the monumentality of
the form. In the 1947 Robinson
house in Williamstown, Massachusetts, the stone fireplace is again
an object in space by itself except
that it has been placed close to a
large window wall in the living
room. A vertical, rectangular
cutout, divided at one point with a
horizontal slab, frames a view of
the site beyond.

By 1941 the strains between
Gropius and Breuer had become
pronounced. Nineteen years older
than Breuer, Gropius had been his
teacher/mentor, encouraged
Breuer to remain at the Bauhaus,
fed him numerous interior design
commissions, helped him set up a
practice in England when Gropius

**Levy House,
Princeton, New
Jersey, 1957.
Marcel Breuer,
Architect, and
Herbert Beckhard,
Associate**
photo: Ben Schnall
© Smithsonian Institution

**Partial west
elevation of
Levy House**
photo: Ben Schnall
© Smithsonian Institution

had moved there earlier, secured the Harvard job for Breuer, and later went into partnership with Breuer in the United States. But by now Breuer had proven his ability to function on his own, and an official—and not altogether amiable—professional break occurred on August 1, 1941. Breuer maintained his practice in Cambridge until 1946 when he moved his office to New York City.

Breuer's first commission independent of Gropius was for the Geller house in Lawrence, Long Island. Breuer was allowed to build the house despite a ban on residential construction during World War II because it was regarded by the U.S. government as an experimental prefabricated house—one, conceivably, that could be adopted on a large scale after the war. Its bi-nuclear plan was seen to be ideal for the postwar family. While Breuer's

house in Lincoln, the Chamberlain Cottage, and the Gropius house on which he collaborated were quickly regarded as exemplars of new Modern domestic architecture, the Geller house was an especially large composition. Also, it made

its appearance in a dense suburban area of otherwise staunchly traditional homes. Each of the house's bi-nuclear rectangular elements is marked by opposing butterfly roof forms that determine, in part, some of the shapes of the windows. Sheathed in cypress boarding, and marked by bands of horizontal windows that maintain privacy and also bring in much natural light, the house has a pronounced sweep across its site.

Lawrence, Long Island, was Beckhard's hometown and he first saw this house—after hearing a combination of derisive and laudatory remarks from townspeople—upon returning from service aboard a Navy aircraft carrier in the Pacific. Beckhard was so inspired by the sight of the Geller house that it confirmed his thoughts

about becoming an architect. Indeed, he regards the Geller house as a catalyst for his chosen career.

Herbert Beckhard was born in Lawrence in 1926 to German immigrant parents. While he points out that his boyhood bedroom was furnished with Bauhaus-influenced pieces, he had no formal exposure to the ideas of the Bauhaus. Many of his relatives and family friends were refugees from Nazi Germany, some of whom furnished their houses with Bauhaus pieces they had brought with them from their former homes.

As a boy Beckhard was encouraged by his mother to paint (she was a talented painter), a discipline in which he excelled. In what is really a rarity with one so talented in the visual arts, Beckhard was also an excellent student in mathematics and science. Though he studied aeronautical engineering at Penn State prior to an almost three-year-long stint in the Navy, Beckhard harbored conscious and subconscious yearnings to be an architect. His encounter with the Geller house was sufficient for those urges to be fully realized. He returned to Penn State and switched his career to architectural engineering. Later, Beckhard enrolled in Princeton where he pursued a graduate degree in architecture. Not unlike Breuer, who left the Academy of Arts when he found the program antiquated and overly theoretical, Beckhard left Princeton after a year when he found the program still entrenched in the traditions of the nineteenth-century Beaux Arts.

Following uninspiring but short-lived architecture jobs with two firms—one Beckhard says was too small and the other too large—Beckhard decided to pursue a position in a firm where he felt that he could learn and grow as an architect. At one point in 1951 he was offered a position by Jose Luis Sert, the eminent Spanish-born architect who had a practice in New York. Upon discovering, however, that Marcel Breuer was also in New York, Beckhard was determined to land a position in his office.

While the forty-nine-year-old Breuer was encouraging to the young Beckhard, he did admit that work was too limited to hire another architect. Echoing Frank Lloyd Wright's experience in securing work at Louis Sullivan's office, Beckhard decided that working for Marcel Breuer at no salary was better than working for other architects at any salary; in fact, he considered the opportunity an extension of his graduate studies. With only six people in the firm (including Breuer and a secretary), Beckhard was able to work immediately in close collaboration with Breuer. The office personnel itself reflected the eclectic, enlightened, and open-minded approach to architecture that Breuer fostered. A rarity in 1951,

Kacmarcik House, St. Paul, Minnesota, 1972. Herbert Beckhard

two of the experienced and established architects were women, Belva Barnes and Beverly Green, the latter among the first black women to practice architecture in America.

Just as Gropius immediately entrusted Breuer with important commissions, so Breuer did with Beckhard. As early as 1952, Beckhard designed the Perry house in New Milford, Connecticut (Breuer allowed Beckhard to "moonlight"). Beckhard collaborated on the five-bedroom vacation house with Bill Landsberg, the chief draftsman in Breuer's office, who upon recognizing Beckhard's enthusiasm told him, "Remember, you don't have to do everything you've learned in this first house—you can save some for the next one." Nonetheless, Beckhard did invest the small house with considerable Breuer-influenced details: colored panels on the exterior, a large fieldstone wall juxtaposed with the light wood framing of the house and the concrete block upon which it rested. But it was on the Levy house in Princeton, New Jersey, that Breuer and Beckhard first worked as collaborators, though in a boss/ employee manner. Built for a Princeton University professor and his wife, the house is noted for its dramatic hovering quality above the site.

There was a special and immediate rapport between the two men. By the mid-1950s Beckhard was an associate of the firm and in 1964 became a full partner. Until

Breuer's retirement in 1979, Beckhard worked together with Breuer on everything from private houses to sizable institutional, governmental, corporate, religious, and industrial projects. Though Breuer worked with each of the four younger partners independently (they, however, never worked with each other), it was on virtually all the houses that he worked exclusively with Beckhard.

This book will examine, chronologically, twenty of the houses in detail, outlining each's design vitals, materials, site features, and client and architect objectives. Most of the houses are collaborative efforts between Breuer and Beckhard; later ones are by Beckhard only or in association with another architect. In numerous interviews I had with Beckhard, often accompanied by visits to the houses together, Beckhard has been able to relay the design history of a house—a perspective, clearly, that no one else has. In some instances, I have spoken to the original clients to hear what they say about the experience of living in a Breuer and Beckhard house, for rarely do

we get to hear from the ultimate consumers of a house. While certainly not dismissing their roles as creators, there is a sense for Breuer and Beckhard that buildings define themselves—given, of course, the requirements of site, client, and budget. As Beckhard has said, "The total architecture— the form, the space, the materials, the relationship of spaces, how they move from one to the other, how a person can use the place— is what is speaking."

All of the following houses are discussed as they were in their original states, free of subsequent changes, and most of the photographs were taken soon after completion. Square footages for houses are calculated so that measurements include the house proper, its walls, and the enclosing walls. Terraces are assigned one-quarter of their actual square-foot value and covered terraces are given one-half of their actual square-foot value. (This is a standard AIA method for calculating the area and cost of a project.) The figure given for each house is the sum of all those parts.

Original House

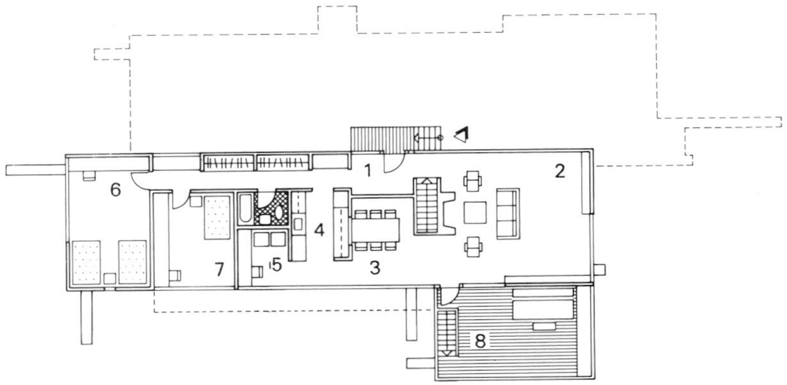

Main Level

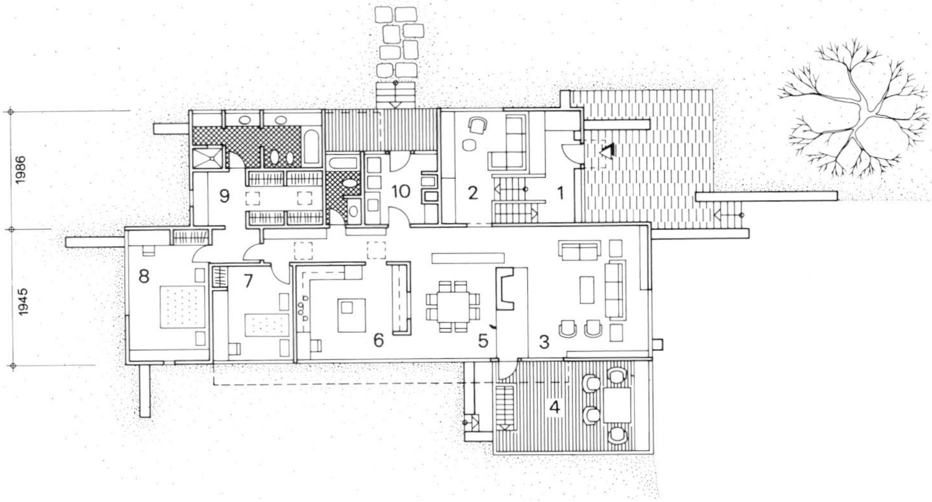

Renovation
1. Entry
2. Den
3. Living
4. Deck
5. Dining
6. Kitchen
7. Child's bedroom
8. Master bedroom
9. Dressing room
10. Utility
11. Second living room
12. Study

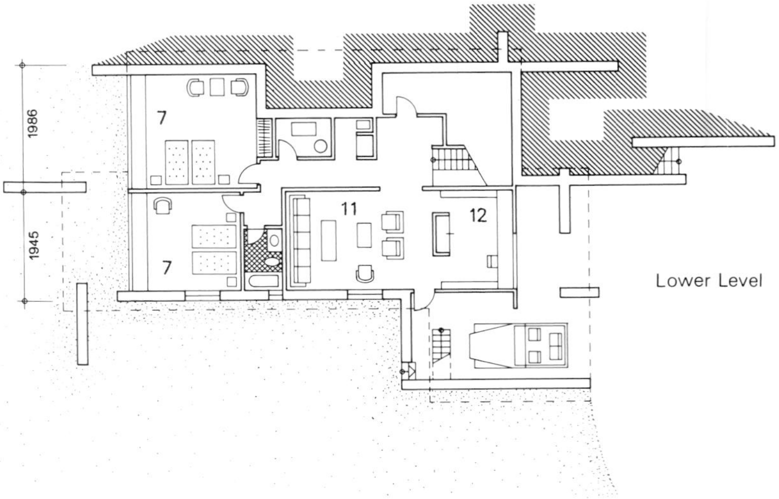

Lower Level

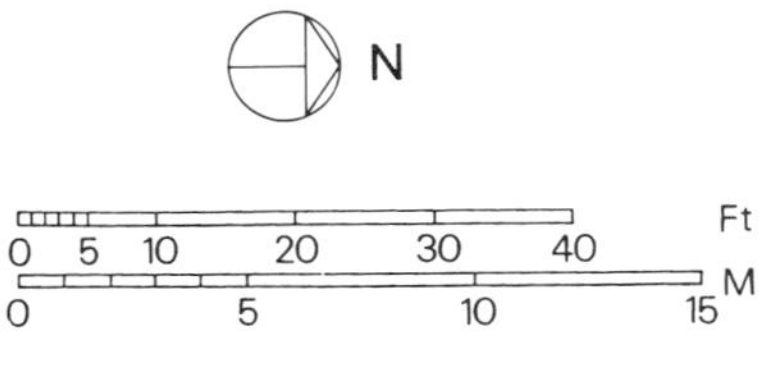

N

Ft
0 5 10   20   30   40
M
0   5   10   15

New Canaan, Connecticut
Original 1945; 2,400 square feet/Marcel Breuer, Architect
Renovation 1986; expanded to 4,200 square feet/Herbert Beckhard, Architect/Andrew Wong, Associate

Original photo
1945, showing the
east elevation. At
the ends, wood
was placed on the
diagonal to assist
in a daring canti-
lever and to add a
visual dynamic to
the structure. Later
occupants would
add awkward steel
columns and posts
to hold up the
cantilevered porch
and the other
far end.

Frank Lloyd Wright's Fallingwater cantilevering over the rushing water, Philip Johnson's pristine Glass House, and the profile of Marcel Breuer's first New Canaan house with its projecting porch, angled roof, and floating form are among the established images of Modern American residential architecture. More so even than Breuer's Geller house of 1945 with its distinctly original butterfly roof and low-slung reach over its site, this house on Sunset Hill Road became an immediate exemplar of Modern architecture. When Beckhard was commissioned in 1986 to nearly double the size of the house he recognized the importance of not violating this

celebrated profile, or the equally distinguished east elevation. Beckhard's reaction, to keep the original house as intact as possible, was an instinctive one—indeed, given his nearly thirty-year association with Breuer, he felt it was an obligation.

Breuer built his decidedly spartan house as a full-time residence for himself and his family. While budgetary concerns certainly limited the scale that it could take, Breuer deliberately designed a house that was compact, modest, and used a limited roster of materials. It was as if the house would represent as a tangible entity his philosophical ideals of what a residence should be—in plan, appear-

ance, and function. With no client stipulations other than his own, Breuer was wholly free to experiment with forms, materials, site placement, and structural details. Rather than having to rigorously accommodate the house to the sloping 2.7-acre site, Breuer separated it from the land, raising it by means of a recessed concrete-block base. The long ends of the house were cantilevered approximately 15 feet, an extraordinary amount for a totally wood structure. Further indulging in his love of structural exploitation and drama (or structure for structure's sake), Breuer cantilevered a generously sized porch held by steel cables out from the main body of the house. A daring and uncannily delicate metal staircase featuring precast concrete treads supported on flat steel straps emerged from the porch to the ground.

The house, essentially a rectangle, is sheathed in vertical cypress wood siding, except at both ends of the east and west facades where the wood siding assists structurally by being installed on the diagonal. Breuer's intent was to reveal this structural dynamic and also create sheer visual variety. It was just this type of structural articulation that would have to serve as decoration. While the north elevation, at which the entrance is placed, was punctuated by only one window, the east elevation had a long expanse of contiguous windows on its upper level; small vertical rectangular slit-like windows were cut into the

Original photo 1945. From the north, the house quickly became one of the most famous and familiar images in residential architecture. The porch is cantilevered by cables which later proved troublesome.
photo: Ezra Stoller ©Esto

Renovated and expanded house 1986. Breuer had already replaced the cable porch supports with a stone wall in 1948. Beckhard adopted that solution by using a series of similar walls at the failed cantilevered ends. Stone facing of the lower level tied all ground-related elements together and permitted the enlarging of lower-level windows. All wood, new and old, was coated with a semi-transparent stain.

photo: Andrew Appell

lower level and in the cantilevers where the wood was on the diagonal. A subtle relationship and harmony was established by the cables supporting the porch and those that held a wood sunscreen device to the facade above the wall of windows.

Within a short time, however, the porch began to sag; Breuer, acknowledged throughout his career for making substantive changes upon clients' requests without complaint or debate, decided to abandon the cable system, despite his affection for its sheer engineering bravado. Using one of his favorite materials, Breuer built a fieldstone wall under the porch as support.

After six years in the house, Breuer built another New Canaan residence for himself and sold this one. (In his lifetime Breuer built four houses for himself.) During the eleven years that the several occupants lived in the house, the

cantilevered ends of the house's long walls, which were actually ten-foot-high wood trusses, began to sag through fatigue stresses. While Breuer might have resorted to using more fieldstone walls as part of the solution, the occupants propped up both of those ends with posts and round steel columns, inappropriate solutions aesthetically and technically.

It was after an eleven-year period in which the house had been rented to a couple that Peter and Trudy Robeck came to it; they later bought the house and continue to live there after nearly thirty years. When the couple came to New Canaan from California in 1956, they had in mind to buy one of the area's old barns and renovate it into a house. As an interim measure, they were looking to rent a house. "When my wife drove me up the driveway to show me this house, I thought, oh my God, what's this? I just wasn't a fan of contemporary architecture, and my wife didn't have an inclination for Modern architecture, either," Mr. Robeck recalls. It was a more-than-century-old weeping hemlock tree on the property that, ultimately, revealed to Mr. Robeck his profound attachment to the house. Though only renters, Mr. Robeck found himself spending considerable time and effort nurturing the growth of the tree. He soon acknowledged that such efforts reflected how he and his wife felt about the house. "I realized then that we were madly in love with this place."

After raising their two children in the relatively small house, the Robecks decided to have the house restored as much as possible to its original state. Also, the rather spartan quarters—a small kitchen, minimal bathrooms, cramped dining area, a difficult-to-locate and less-than-inviting entryway—had become tiring and the Robecks embarked on a major expansion and upgrading of the facilities. Aware of Beckhard's long affiliation with Breuer, the houses he had designed solely, and the addition he had made in 1977 to Breuer's second New Canaan home, the Robecks entrusted him with the task. It was a commission that involved remaining true to Breuer's original vision and philosophy, as well as accommodating the very different and real needs of the clients.

Beckhard attached the new expansion parallel to the rear facade and recessed it at both ends. In so doing, three of the principal facades remain essentially untouched. Because the original house juts out from the new addition, the famous north and east elevations are not affected. The angle of the roof of the new wing is reversed from the original, resulting in a butterfly or reverse pitch configuration vaguely reminiscent of the original Geller house. By positioning the roof this way the house is allowed to grow in a natural and probably historically correct way.

While the old entrance, as the Robecks describe it, "felt more

What had been
an almost hidden
entrance is replaced
by an ample
entryway reached
through a series of
low stone walls and
entrance terrace.
photo: Andrew Appell

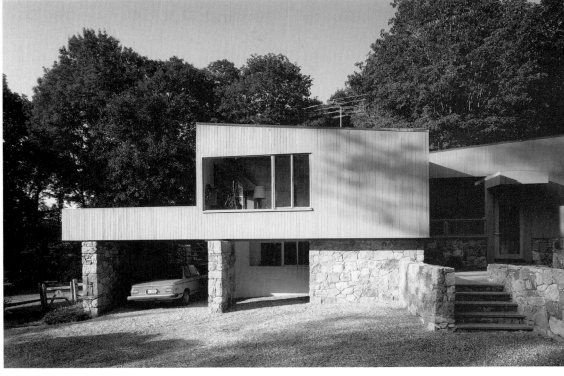

like a back door," the function of the new entry is unmistakable. The more visible entry is reached much more directly from a raised terrace, and a series of low fieldstone walls further articulate the approach. The improvised posts and steel columns have been removed and replaced by geometrically juxtaposed fieldstone walls. To ensure that the cypress wood siding of the new wing matched that of the existing, all wood new and old was coated with a semi-transparent stain.

The exposed foundation wall on the east elevation is now faced with fieldstone, which draws attention to the lower level and creates cohesion among the old and new lower-level elements. In the original incarnation, the understated lower level could easily be regarded as mere storage space. Because this level now features actual living spaces, Beckhard added windows to bring in more light and to capture views from within.

To anyone who was familiar with the original, almost haphazard entryway, Beckhard's is spacious, inviting, and room-like. It is also true to Breuer's palette with its bluestone flooring, Breuer-blue door, interior stone walls, and distinctive window shapes. Where the former entrance used to be is now a service entrance. Within the reconfigured entry a new interior staircase leads both down and up to the main living areas (a split-level arrangement). At the top landing is a sitting area/study that opens onto the main corridor of the house from which rooms are accessed. By eliminating a former bathroom, the kitchen and dining area were enlarged. Within the new wing is a full guest bathroom and an expansive dressing area and bathroom for the master bedroom. As postwar families have aged, it seems that they insist on having more ample dressing and sleeping areas and more luxurious bathrooms. What was suitable for families in the 1950s had suddenly become dated.

Other interior details that

The New England fieldstone walls are arranged in a diametrically opposed fashion. The lattice sun screen is maintained and even extended to include a narrow window at the master bedroom.
photo: Andrew Appell

have given the house the authenticity insisted upon by both the Robecks and Beckhard include the repainting of interior walls—mostly white with occasional Breuer-blue accents, as in the living room wall, and another favorite Breuer color like yellow in the downstairs sitting room. The Breuer-blue wall at one end of the living room is among the first things one sees when entering the room. The piercing color was devised by Breuer during his Bauhaus days. It is a mixture of ultramarine and cobalt blues; and more than any form, plan, or material, it immediately makes Breuer's presence known. Adopted by Beckhard in houses

he designed on his own, the intense color appears on doors, walls, panels, and garage doors in several other houses.

Cypress boarding as was used on the original ceilings was used again for the new ones. Because the main interior corridor is now completely contained within the house and no longer able to receive light from windows, Beckhard cut two skylights into the roof to bring in natural light. A 1950s favorite material, sisal matting, instead of the wall-to-wall carpeting that had been installed later, was put down in the living and dining areas. By eliminating a dining room wall and an interior staircase Beckhard was able to

maintain the linear arrangement of rooms, while also significantly enlarging the dining room and creating a plan that feels even more open.

While the view of the land remains in a sense the central visual object, from within the house the only other element competing for attention is a built one, the fireplace. It acts as more of a visual barrier than a literal one between the living and dining areas. While later Breuer and Beckhard fireplaces often became exuberant and highly sculptural in form, this one is more modest, but powerful nonetheless. Comprised of painted white brick that culminates abruptly at an angle as it meets

The new entry is a room of its own. A sitting room/ office is at the top of the split-level arrangement. A second stair run provides direct access to the lower level.
photo: Andrew Appell

The restored living room utilizes the original materials of the 1945 design. Notable are the white painted fireplace, sisal matting floor, and Breuer-blue end wall combined with book shelves.
photo: Andrew Appell

the wood ceiling, it includes a vertical rectangular cutout that lessens this heavy element and shows Breuer's sculptural concerns for the fireplace.

The enlarged main deck off the living room remains a much-used exterior living space. And though from the main living floor one is clearly aware of being above the ground, there is no sense of uneasiness. For one thing, the staircase that Breuer had cut into the deck leading to the ground is crucial. From within the house the staircase reminds people that they can always get to the ground easily. The floating nature of the house allows for not only the preservation of the natural lay of the land but also a way to live with that landscape and see it in its entirety from every main room. Mr. Robeck remarks that the overall experience is akin to "living in a tree house. Every place you look out there's a marvelous vista, but I never feel remote from the earth."

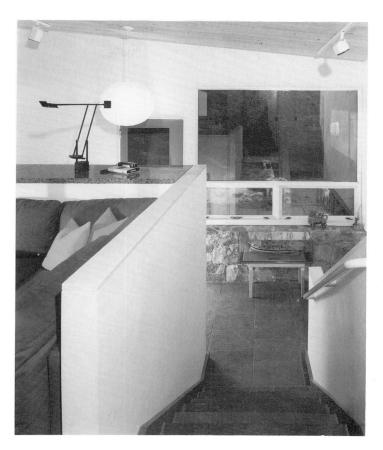

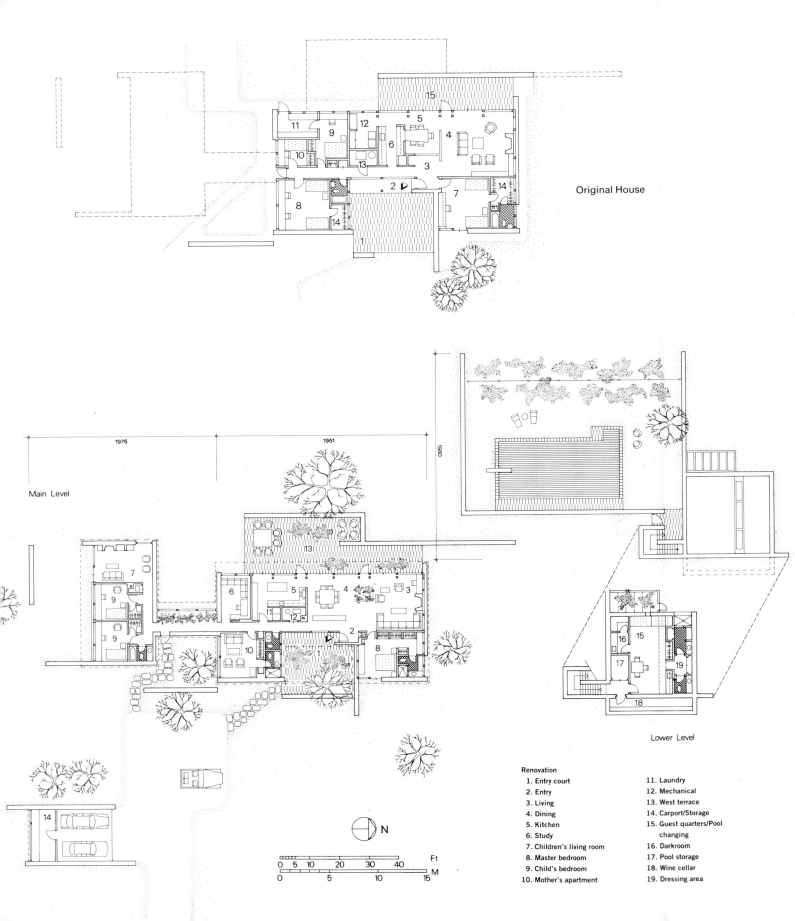

Original House

Main Level

1976   1951   1980

Lower Level

Renovation

1. Entry court
2. Entry
3. Living
4. Dining
5. Kitchen
6. Study
7. Children's living room
8. Master bedroom
9. Child's bedroom
10. Mother's apartment
11. Laundry
12. Mechanical
13. West terrace
14. Carport/Storage
15. Guest quarters/Pool changing
16. Darkroom
17. Pool storage
18. Wine cellar
19. Dressing area

N

0 5 10   20   30   40   Ft
0   5   10   15   M

Breuer/ Bratti House

New Canaan, Connecticut
Original 1951; 3,000 square feet; Marcel Breuer, Architect
First addition 1979; second addition 1982; 4,600 square feet; Herbert Beckhard, Architect/Robert Kupies, Associate

From the east, or entrance facade, the original Breuer house in 1951 before alterations were made. The free-standing fieldstone wall at left would become the screening wall for a new additional courtyard.
photo: Ben Schnall

It was during a year-long house-sitting stint that Beckhard came to fully understand the phenomena that characterized life in a Breuer house; up until then they had been more professional, abstract notions than actual experienced ones. The year was 1953 and Beckhard had been working in Breuer's New York office for only a short time. Upon receiving the commission for the UNESCO headquarters in Paris, Breuer found it necessary to re-locate to that city for a year during the design phase of the project and he asked his young employee to house sit in his New Canaan home.

Among the defining dynamics of the house that the young Beckhard came to appreciate was the interplay between exterior and interior spaces. A courtyard that captured simultaneously the sense of interior and exterior space, a terrace that extended out from and along the length of the house's private side, and the use of full-height glass walls contrasted by full-height stone ones became especially memorable phenomena when living with them daily. Beckhard readily admits that a good part of his education as an architect came from living in the house. "I had been looking at Breuer houses, reading about them, studying them, drawing them, but I had never lived in that kind of environment before." Beckhard could not have guessed at the time that many years later he would be responsible for reconfiguring and significantly enlarging the house.

In 1945 Breuer built a house for his family on Sunset Hill Road in New Canaan that quickly became an exemplar of Modern American domestic architecture. After less than five years in the house, Breuer decided rather impetuously to build a new house in the town for his family which

included his wife, Connie, and his son, Thomas (a daughter, Cesca, would be born later). Beckhard recalls Breuer saying the reason he wanted to build again was that he was inspired by the great beauty of the new site, though the Sunset Hill Road site was equally distinguished. Numerous commissions at the time brought in more income for Breuer and, given the rather Spartan facilities of the first house, he might have decided it was time for something more comfortable. Perhaps more pointedly, the new house allowed Breuer the chance to experiment with new forms and materials. In a short time, the new house he created, along with the former, would become regular pilgrimage sites for scores of young architects who came to New Canaan in the 1950s to see the several notable Modern houses that were built there. Though New Canaan was and remains a conservative, wealthy suburb of New York, the town became the site for some highly innovative designs—in addition to the two Breuer residences and two other Breuer houses, there was Philip Johnson's Glass House and notable houses by Eliot Noyes, John Johansen, and Landis Gores, among others.

While Breuer's first house daringly rose above its site, the new house adamantly rested on the earth. In so doing Breuer was able to use stone, which because of its sheer weight needs to rest on the ground. With its entrance facade virtually all stone, the

The extensions to the house remain true to the spirit of the original. A new children's wing is seen at left.
photo: Nick Wheeler

Beckhard changed elements of the original entrance courtyard. A free beam, an original feature, serves to capture and define outdoor space. Beckhard inserted a fixed window in the brick wall by the entry where originally there had been a series of sliding frosted glass doors.
photo: Nick Wheeler

house has the initial presence of a solid object. Another of Breuer's favorite materials, bluestone, was used on the interior floors, at the entry court, and on a rear terrace. The heating systems presented another chance to experiment. Because the entire floor rests on a slab on grade, Breuer was able to install a radiant heating system in which coils are embedded in the slab. Breuer had never done this before and it was a relatively new technology at the time. With this application interior spaces can be free of clumsy and hard-to-clean radiators, convectors, or grilles. Also, the absence of such devices allowed for floor-to-ceiling panes of glass and for furniture to be placed more freely.

While the boxy geometry of the Sunset Hill Road house made for a sharply defined envelope, this house exploits the idea of independent, extended planes. In many cases, full planes of solids (fieldstone walls) are juxtaposed with full planes of glass. On a few elevations high-up horizontal windows have brick or stone under them. But neither the glass nor the solid walls ever turn a corner; they are met instead by their foil. Though this was a feature that Breuer had previously used—as early as 1936 with his Gane Pavilion—here it could be implemented on an especially large scale. Breuer and Beckhard's frequent desire for houses to have a virtually solid entrance facade and a highly fenestrated rear one is as apparent here as in any of their houses. With the

exception of the bedrooms at the south and the master bedroom facing north, all of the principal windows of the house face west, at the rear, while the entrance facade is largely closed off from the street.

This is also the first house in which Breuer fashioned an entrance courtyard. While courtyards in later Breuer and Beckhard houses are prominent outdoor living spaces, here the ante space is simply meant to accent the entry to the house. The space is small and alluring, but never intended for activities like barbecuing or sitting outdoors. A free beam that crosses the space and continues the roof line does much to capture additional outdoor space. This characteristic of carrying a roof or suggesting that it continues over outdoor spaces becomes more pronounced in several later houses. Though the court was defined by bluestone paving and a minimal, low, sitting-height fieldstone wall, because it remained wholly open to the front lawn the court lacked the privacy needed to feel or function like an outdoor room.

As for the plan, the single-story house allowed Breuer to further explore the idea of having living quarters removed from sleeping ones. Though he had long separated bedrooms from living areas, he had not so emphatically separated bedrooms from bedrooms—that is, children's from adults'. The master bedroom, situated in the northeast corner of the house, is immediately ac-

On the west side, the original wall of windows contrasts with the largely solid new wing, though the passageway linking the two elements is fully fenestrated. The enlarged terrace is defined by a series of fieldstone walls.
photo: Nick Wheeler

A series of walls screen the swimming pool from the house. At the lower left is the stairway leading down into the submerged guest house. The north elevation of the Breuer house with its strip of high-placed windows remains unchanged.
photo: Nick Wheeler

cessible upon entering the house, while other bedrooms are reached through a corridor running from north to south. A sliding glass door facing the street brings in morning light; a large evergreen tree planted in front maintains privacy from the street as well as the solidity of the front elevation.

For Marcel (who always went by "Lajko," which means "Louis" in Hungarian) and his wife, Connie, who rarely, if ever, entertained on a large scale and who coveted privacy, the house was ideally suited for their needs. But later in life when he decided that a city apartment and a Cape Cod retreat were enough to manage, Breuer sold it in 1976. It was a painful decision for the Breuers.

The new residents, Nancy and Gerald Bratti, entertained frequently on a grand scale, were used to living in a large house, and had two children and Mrs. Bratti's widowed mother living with them. (Mr. Bratti was the head of a stone business and the house clearly had an immediate appeal to him.) Given the particulars of the new clients, it was clear that the house would need considerable adjustments. Like the Robecks, the residents of the first Breuer New Canaan home who later entrusted Beckhard with the design of an addition, the Brattis, too, felt that only he would be capable of producing a sensitive, creative, and yet contextual redesign.

Well aware of what the house represented to Breuer, Beckhard

At dusk, the effect
of the window walls
becomes especially
pronounced.
photo: Nick Wheeler

felt an especially great responsibility to honor his former mentor and partner as well as to satisfy the Brattis' requirements. According to Beckhard, Nancy Bratti was an especially involved, responsive, and knowledgeable client. She understood the importance of keeping the integrity of the house and that additional elements should be independent compositions intimately related nonetheless to the original. Beckhard recalls his association with her as being among the best architect/owner collaborations of his career.

The new wing is positioned at the south end of the house and set back slightly from the line of the entrance facade. Like the original facade, the wall here is solid while a lower fieldstone wall set on the site marks off the boundary of a second, newly created courtyard. As for the existing entrance courtyard, Beckhard extended the extant minimal fieldstone wall so

that the space becomes more closed off and private. Grass, trees, and other landscaping replace the completely paved surface, while an informal path leads to the front door.

While the separate wing remains distinct from the original house, the materials that comprise it and the types of windows used remain true to the original. The wing is attached to the original house by a passageway faced on the street side with stone and on the rear with glass; in so doing the play of solid versus glazed long elevations remains. However, at the wing's rear or west elevation, with the exception of a large window in what is the children's living room, the facade is solid, which counters the wall of windows of the original. Beckhard did not want the wing to compete for attention with the original, so all of the windows of the bedrooms and children's living room face south instead of west. In fact, the original bedrooms were oriented south.

An important exterior change involved the replacing of a floor-to-ceiling-length sliding frosted window at the entrance. In its place a white painted brick wall was erected—a material and treatment that already appeared on the house—into which was inserted a clear pane of glass. Upon entering the entrance courtyard, the visitor can literally look through the house to the terrace at the back. This rear terrace was enlarged considerably and is articulated by a series of low juxtaposed fieldstone walls.

Though Breuer didn't feel the need for one, the Brattis did want a garage, and Beckhard's solution honors a predilection both he and Breuer have which is to separate the garage from the house. To do so ensures that every approach to the house is an extended and pronounced one. A subtle design feature of the garage here is that the two fieldstone walls that encase it are each extended out in opposite directions from the actual edges of the structure. The building then becomes longer, further extending the horizontal pull of the house across the site.

Beckhard's interior changes were dramatic and followed a kind of domino effect. Though the living and dining areas were an open plan, a fixed semi-transparent bamboo screen did separate the two areas; it was removed to enlarge the living room. Mrs. Bratti and her mother needed a kitchen where they could indulge in their love of cooking and that could accommodate the preparation of food for large numbers of guests. The original galley kitchen was subsumed into a relocated dining area. A new kitchen with ample counter space and an island counter/eating unit was fashioned from a space formerly occupied by a laundry area, storage space, and a bedroom. The remaining space not used for the new kitchen became an office/study.

In the front of the house, what had been Tom Breuer's bedroom was turned into an apartment for Mrs. Bratti's mother, complete

A view toward the pool and guest house. The array of low stone walls allows for open views onto the pool and the landscape beyond. The labyrinth-like arrangement of walls is reminiscent of ancient ruins.
photo: Nick Wheeler

with a new bathroom. The stone wall that closes off the courtyard onto which this room looks also becomes an important screening wall from the road. The master bedroom was actually reduced in size to allow for additional storage and closet space and to increase the size of the bathroom. For his own use, Breuer felt that minimally sized bathrooms were sufficient, though some of his clients feel otherwise. Breuer also had a pen-

chant for making bedrooms modest in size and spare as a way to encourage people to use the more open and inviting living spaces.

To accommodate Mrs. Bratti's avocation as a gardener, two large skylights were cut into the roof approximately over the midpoint of the living/dining area. Here groupings of hanging and potted indoor plants receive sunlight throughout the day. As in the Laaff house, a horizontal band of

clerestory-like windows runs the length of the wall where the fireplace is situated, bringing in light while maintaining privacy. Unlike other more elaborately sculpted fireplaces, this one, essentially a simple box, is made of white painted brick, with an exposed terra-cotta flue emerging from the top. Despite all of this natural light, the entire house was further lightened by replacing the wood ceilings that had darkened with

Breuer remained conspicuously absent during Beckhard's dealings with the Brattis, perhaps because he found the alterations on his beloved house a bit painful. Because of that Beckhard felt the pressure even more to maintain the very ethos of the house. Upon completion, the Brattis invited the Beckhards and the Breuers to lunch. It was the first time Breuer had seen the changes and Beckhard remembers with great relief and pride how Breuer, ever reticent in his praise, said simply to Beckhard, "I appreciate what you've done." Coming from Breuer, such a minimal response was a full-scale endorsement.

In the remodeling, Beckhard removed the bamboo screen separating living from dining, installed new wood on the ceilings, and had two skylights cut into the roof. The line of windows above the top of the fireplace and the bluestone flooring are original features of the house.
photo: Nick Wheeler

age with light-hued wood from Finland.

When the Brattis subsequently decided to add a pool and guest house, Beckhard felt that the site already contained as many visible elements as it could handle and he did not want to encroach on it any further. Not wanting the house to ramble on indefinitely on the site, Beckhard submerged both the pool and guest house to a level considerably below that of the house. The pool is positioned sufficiently far off to the north so that from the living/dining area it is not even visible. Four-foot-high safety walls (a town requirement) made of fieldstone are all that are seen from within the house. The

terrain to the west of the pool slopes down abruptly, and within dense shrubbery devised by Beckhard the remaining safety fence (chain link there) is concealed.

The guest house is completely underground, lit by a continuous barrel-vault skylight that courses its roof. From the outside, the guest house and pool complex appears like a labyrinth, or as Beckhard calls it, "a newly created ruin." The 600-square-foot structure, containing sleeping and dining quarters, kitchenette, dark room, wine cellar, and storage area, is reached by a stairway that winds its way down amid fieldstone walls.

What had been a
galley kitchen became
a full-sized room in a
new location.
photo: Nick Wheeler

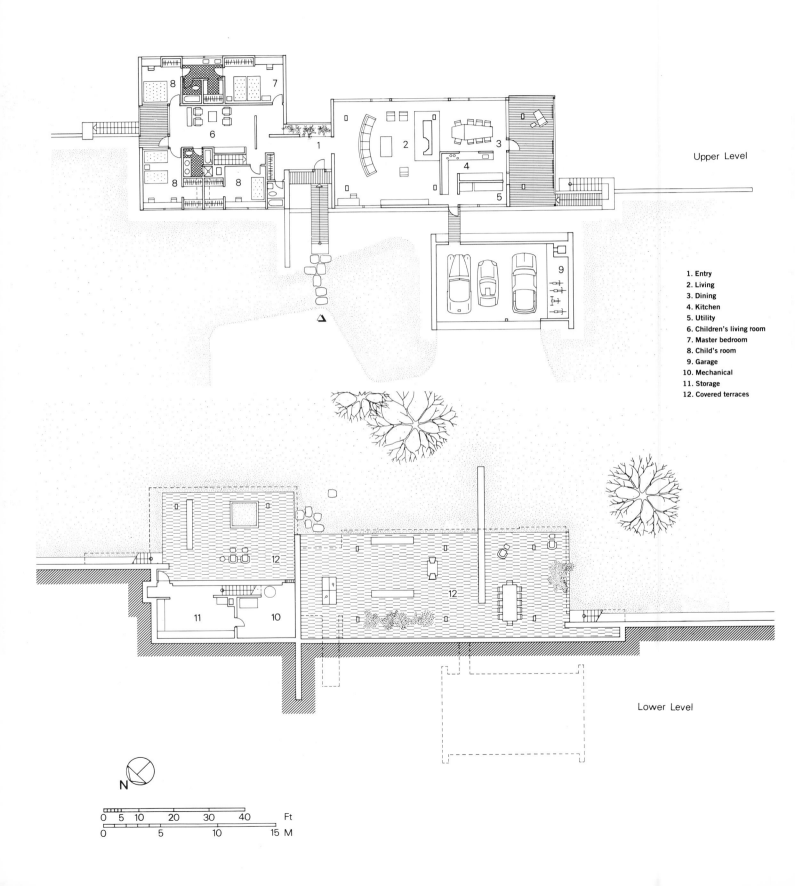

Upper Level

1. Entry
2. Living
3. Dining
4. Kitchen
5. Utility
6. Children's living room
7. Master bedroom
8. Child's room
9. Garage
10. Mechanical
11. Storage
12. Covered terraces

Lower Level

N

0 5 10   20   30   40   Ft

0   5   10   15 M

Duluth, Minnesota, 1954
Approximately 4,200 square feet
Marcel Breuer, Architect/Herbert Beckhard, Associate

From the entrance
side, the house has
a brief relationship to
the ground. But the
steep site is revealed
by the gap beneath
the element of the
house next to the
garage.
photo: Ezra Stoller
© Esto

"Where there's structure it is always good to express it," Marcel Breuer said of this house in an interview with *Time* magazine in 1956. While the visual expression of structure is fundamental to many Breuer and Beckhard buildings, here it becomes impossible to separate structure from aesthetics. This is among the architects' most famous houses, in part because it manages to encompass so many of the key characteristics that define their houses: a conspicuously exposed structural system, a preoccupation with solar control, a play between being an earthbound and a gravity-defying structure, an established contrast between a spare understated entrance facade and a strongly articulated rear one, and a binuclear plan that also helps foster the phenomenon of entering a house at the front and immediately winding up at the back.

Because the house is built on a slope that rises above Lake Superior, Breuer and Beckhard were able to build two kinds of structures—one that is firmly rooted on the ground and another that is reticent to make contact with it. In fact, given the architects' penchant for houses that simultaneously embrace and shun the earth, the very problems of the site were welcoming ones. As an architecture without rules, Modern houses like this one can take any shape they want and the structure that allows them to do so is to be highlighted, not concealed.

On the lake side the house cantilevers out over the grassy slope, while on the entrance side it appears firmly rooted to the ground. The prominent three-car garage wing, two walls of which are of fieldstone, hugs the earth while the bedroom wing to the left of the entrance is also connected directly to grade. But an entrance ramp and a startling gap between a re-

taining wall and the living wing element of the house adjacent to the garage reveals the house's brief relationship to the ground. A second exterior bridge suspended by stainless-steel cables links the garage to the kitchen/service entrance. Both bridges are nautical in feel–appropriate given the lake setting.

A kind of nether zone or alleyway-like space that results between the garage and the actual house is an intriguing one. It is neither an exterior living space nor an endemic part of the landscape. The lane is revealed when one crosses either of the two bridges. The space seems an appropriate synthesis of the natural environment and the built, architectural one. Furthermore, there is a great sense of drama when traversing either bridge for it is a unique way to enter a house. Like any suspension bridge, one is aware of its give and even slight sway. The architects' interest in announcing the entrance to a house is carried to its pinnacle here.

Though from the entrance elevation the house appears relatively modest in scale and detail, much of the house's structural system is revealed. It is especially discernible because the roadway is slightly elevated, so that from it one looks down on to the house. Two laminated wood girders stretch across the living wing part of the roof, which is suspended by means of intermediate steel hangers from the girders. The floor framing is supported by similar

The entrance is reached via a suspended bridge that immediately reveals the floating nature of the house. Another bridge (not seen here) links the earthbound garage to the kitchen. One of the roof's laminated beams crosses the entrance area.
photo: Ezra Stoller © Esto

The fireplace on the lower level is open at both ends, lessening the monumentality of the form and maintaining the sense that the space is a wholly open one. A low fieldstone wall suggests a boundary with the outside. The steel pins on which the cantilevered house rests emerge several inches above the ground.
photo: Ezra Stoller © Esto

longitudinal wood girders that become visible on the underside of the house at the rear. In both cases, the wood girders are laminated, not only as a way to draw attention to them but for reasons of strength. The lamination minimizes the movement of the wood through shrinkage and swelling.

As the front facade subtly hints at the kinds of technical wonders that characterize the house, the rear and west facades brazenly announce them. The house is supported by means of laminated wood posts. The drama is heightened by narrow steel pins welded to metal shoes that emerge from the wood posts a few inches from the ground. Though these pins reach down to foundations and then to bedrock, their ability to support the house above seems uncanny. Sheer structural intrigue is not the only reason the wood does not meet the ground. By separating the wood from the grade, the material is immune to the rotting effects of moisture.

Aside from the six widely spaced wood posts and low-rising, geometrically juxtaposed fieldstone walls, the only other element beneath the house that reaches from ground to roof is a sculpted concrete fireplace, whose exposed board forms take on opposing horizontal and vertical expressions. Within the house the fireplace is rectangular and bush-hammered so that the lively stone aggregates are revealed, while on the exterior it translates into a smaller fireplace with angled planes of poured

concrete. With its hearth open on both sides, the fireplace on the terrace below the house becomes a kind of outdoor window when looked at head-on from either end; the window effect hints that the space is both an outdoor and an indoor one. Indeed, the whole covered terrace epitomizes how an outdoor space can be made to resemble an interior one. Though open to the lawn beyond, a low freestanding wall establishes a boundary with the uncovered portion. Grass is allowed to grow between the flagstones—it suggests that even though nature is allowed to overtake the built site, the space is, nonetheless, one protected from the elements.

Because the rear of the house faces southeast with an open expanse to the lake, the house is bathed in sunlight year-round. Sun control for the glass walls is achieved by two devices. An overhang of open, horizontally placed wood slats is mounted below the top of the window sections (unlike, for instance, the Robeck house, where such devices meet the top edge of the windows). Vertical panels of heat- and light-reflecting glass rise above the roof line and are placed parallel to the window walls but in front of them. From within the house, the remaining section of the windows above the panel of wood slats are in effect clerestory windows. Since the deliberate application of ornament to buildings is anathema to Breuer and Beckhard, one has to believe that these sun-shading devices are

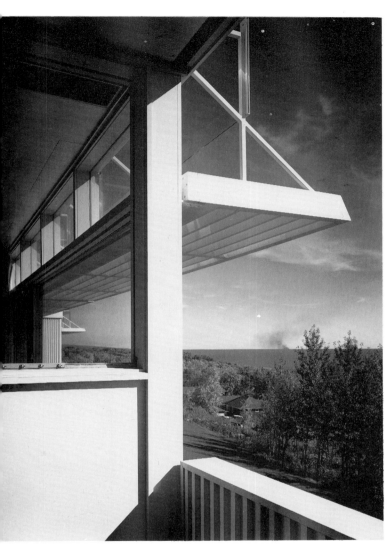

From the west
porch, the section
of windows above
the sun screen
becomes a kind of
clerestory above an
uninterrupted
window wall.
photo: Ezra Stoller
© Esto

The rear, or south
elevation, shows
how the house is
cantilevered above
its steep site.
Though purely
functional, the sun
screen devices
become important
aesthetic elements.
photo: Ezra Stoller © Esto

somewhat elaborate in form because of their essential function. Yet, by nature of their very technicality they become aesthetic, perhaps even ornamental elements; and it is hard to imagine that the house would be as visually compelling without them.

Two porches, one on either end of the house reached by exterior staircases, further open up the volume of the house. They also promote immediate indoor/outdoor access. The staircases themselves are open compositions. Precast concrete treads are simply cantilevered from the stone wall and left riserless; the unembellished, open handrail has no vertical supports except at the landings (building codes today would not allow for this). One porch runs the full width of the house while the other is more of a notch within the envelope of the structure. One side of the larger porch has four sliding panels comprised of traditional Bauhaus colors—yellow, red, white, and gray. They are set on a track and can be stacked off to a side or spread out to block the setting sun. Though the laminated wood and fieldstones are resonant with hues, the panels are especially startling splashes of color.

Early on in his career Breuer himself labeled those houses binuclear that separated living zones from sleeping ones—but Beckhard says that he seldom if ever heard Breuer use that term later on. Here all living areas are situated apart from the bedrooms; this becomes evident immediately upon entering

the house. After traversing the entrance ramp, the visitor enters a glass-enclosed foyer with random slabs of bluestone as flooring. With its wall of glass facing the lake, the entrance area makes one keenly aware that the house is elevated above the terrain. To the right is the living and dining area, separated by the fireplace and a combined kitchen and laundry facility. In this house all living areas are situated in one zone while bedrooms are in another. While this placement is apparent in many Breuer and Beckhard houses, sometimes the master suite is placed within the living areas, resulting in houses with an adult and a children's zone. Here the bedrooms are grouped together because the client, June Alworth, a young widow, at the time wanted to be in close contact with her three small children. (Not long after completion of the house Mrs. Alworth remarried to Robert Starkey.) All four bedrooms revolve around an ample family/children's living room, dually lit by a skylight and a window onto a porch. Be-

The west porch
with its four sliding
panels that can
regulate sunlight.
The stairway leading
to the porch is com-
prised of precast
concrete pieces that
are cantilevered from
the stone wall.
photo: Ezra Stoller © Esto

The porch on the
east side of the house
is accessible from the
family/children's
room, and has its own
exterior staircase.
photo: Ezra Stoller
© Esto

The bush-hammered
fireplace is a contrast
of rectangular forms,
a pass-through, a
sculptural niche, and
the fireplace itself.
photo: Ezra Stoller
© Esto

cause there is no sensation of corridors, one moves easily from
space to space. Uninterrupted expanses free of corridors and walls
within and below the house were a
design precedent.

The house is clearly an edi-
fice of horizontal expression. The
only element that diverges from
that strong linear quality is the
seemingly free-flowing, sensuously
shaped driveway. Though the site
could have easily allowed for a
simple straight driveway, Breuer
and Beckhard wanted to develop
some contrast with the straight-
line geometry of the building. Indeed, the architects have a tendency to use free-flowing landscape forms as a foil to the linear
discipline of their buildings.

There is a great sense of daring about this house. Rather than
simply demurring to the steep, almost unwieldy site, the house
challenges it by literally rising
above it. At as many places as possible structure is wholly revealed,
so there are no secrets. Exuberant
forms, materials, and objects are
exploited, like the colorful sliding
porch panels, sculpted exterior
fireplace, and various fieldstone
walls on the site. There is nothing
passive about the building; yet,
despite all that it embodies, the
house does not become over-
expressed, overbuilt, or immodest.

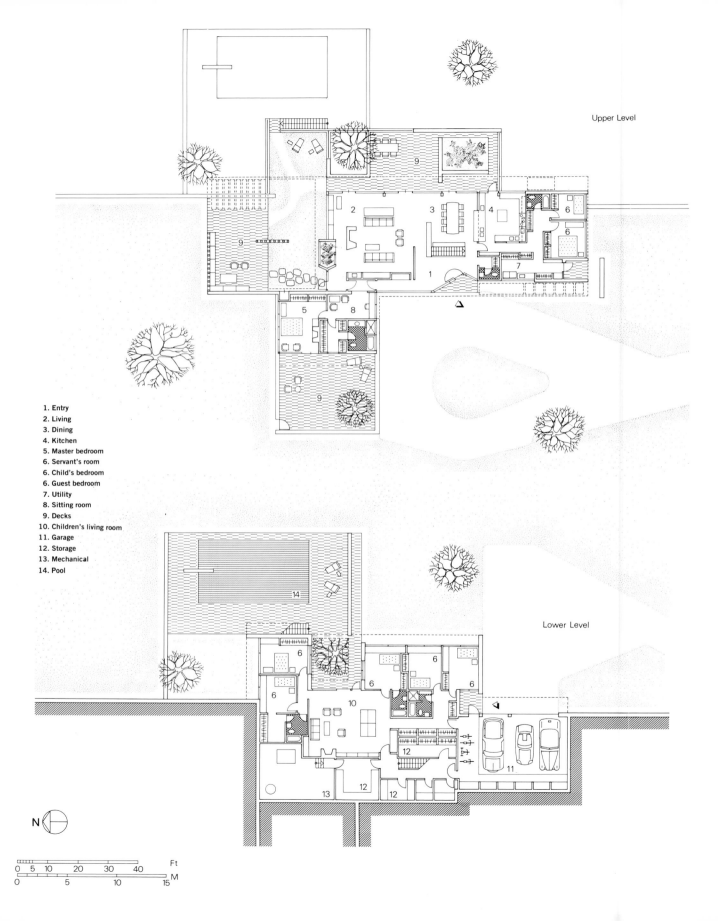

Upper Level

Lower Level

1. Entry
2. Living
3. Dining
4. Kitchen
5. Master bedroom
6. Servant's room
6. Child's bedroom
6. Guest bedroom
7. Utility
8. Sitting room
9. Decks
10. Children's living room
11. Garage
12. Storage
13. Mechanical
14. Pool

N

0 5 10   20   30   40 Ft
0   5   10   15 M

Gagarin I House

Litchfield, Connecticut, 1955
Approximately 12,200 square feet
Marcel Breuer, Architect/Herbert Beckhard, Associate

At the west, or entrance elevation, the house appears to be relatively modest in size, an objective of both owner and architects. At left is a wall that forms part of the master bedroom courtyard. A play of light and shadow is produced by the roof overhang seen at right.
photo: Ben Schnall

"Breuer very much wanted and sought out our ideas in a general aspect—how we wanted to live in the house, how we would use it— but he was also very much involved in all of the relatively small details," recalls Andy Gagarin. "He always studied the details and came up with imaginative solutions. And for a great architect who could have easily taken the route that 'I know what I'm doing,' that was pretty remarkable." Though this sizable house was a collaboration between Breuer and Beckhard, in 1975 Beckhard would be the sole architect for a very small house Mr. Gagarin would build in Big Sur, California.

Beckhard, who at the time was a newly appointed young associate in Breuer's office, remembers Andy and Jamie Gagarin as clients intimately involved in the design process. For Beckhard, this was the first consequential project for which he was respon-

sible. Upon completing the schematic design drawings for the house and presenting them with Breuer to the client, Beckhard, with youthful enthusiasm, was convinced that the drawings were "perfect"; indeed they had been fully endorsed by Breuer. The plan required one to circulate through the living room to get to the master bedroom, but the client preferred a more direct and private route. Without hesitation Breuer drew a diagonal line that extended the main entry, and in so doing created a whole new corridor and entrance elevation. Initially unsettled by that maneuver because he thought his "perfect" plan had been destroyed, Beckhard witnessed Breuer's legendary resourcefulness in being able to readily accommodate even something as dramatic as that change. Beckhard learned at that point that an architect has to be willing to adjust and turn what seems to be a

disadvantage into an advantage. Breuer's change in the plan resulted in a diagonal front entrance, among the strongest design dynamics of the house.

Previously, the Gagarins had been living in a traditional style Georgian house. The fact that this house, by virtue of its being Modern, could feature uninterrupted expanses of glass to capture views of the hills beyond was an exhilarating phenomenon for the clients. Breuer and Beckhard, as always with their houses, fostered a natural and intimate relationship between exterior and interior with multiple terraces, enclosed courts, and, in this case, even a small interior greenhouse that is an integral part of the living room. Aside from the requisite for full views, perhaps the most general criterion of the client was that the house be large but not appear so, especially to arriving visitors. As the family's sole residence, it needed to accommodate four young children, while ensuring that adults had privacy and the ability to entertain on a grand scale. Indeed, from the entrance side, the 12,200-square-foot house appears quite modest in size. Yet, from the rear, or downhill side, the house becomes an impressively large and elongated two-story structure with substantial terraces and fieldstone walls that extend into the landscape. The building has a pronounced, elegant horizontal sweep across the site.

With that early stroke of Breuer's pencil the master bed-

room suite became an especially pronounced, separate wing of the house, complete with its own large private courtyard. Leading into the master bedroom is a sitting room/ study that in turn leads to the bathroom and dressing area. One door separates the wing from the entrance foyer while another leads into the living room; adjacent to that door is another leading out to a grassy terrace.

Besides the master bedroom wing, there are two other distinct zones on the first floor. As in virtually all Breuer and Beckhard houses, the living and dining areas act as one expansive space with the kitchen part of, or a semi-part of, that same space. Here, however, the kitchen remains distinct, situated in what is in effect a wing with two maids' rooms, pantry, laundry, and storage facilities. Downstairs, which becomes grade level at the rear as the house is built into a hillside, are the four children's bedrooms, guest quarters, and children's playroom/ family room. In many of the architects' houses this playroom/family room, which doubles as a circulation space, is often situated wholly within the house, but here there is direct access to the outside with its yard and swimming pool.

Both inside and outside the house is an especially rich com-

At the rear the house is a two-story structure. Fieldstone walls on either side extend the house along the site. The riserless steps of the exterior staircase are cantilevered from the fieldstone wall.
photo: Ben Schnall

North elevation. The upstairs terrace is actually the roof of the first level. Freestanding wood screens are both functional supports and suggestive walls that determine outdoor "rooms." As with most of the architects' pools, this one is out of sight from the principal living spaces.
photo: Ben Schnall

bination and juxtaposition of materials. The entrance area, the corridor leading to the master bedroom wing, and a part of the living room are paved with brick; the rest of the flooring is teak wood. The shift of floor materials is subtle, since there is similarity among colors. Structural beams spanning the living and dining area are exposed, but the steel members are encased in teak wood. Ceilings throughout are of dark-brown rough textured cork that carries to the underside of the exterior roof overhangs; such a subtle carrying of material from inside spaces to outside ones establishes an intimate relationship between the exterior and interior aspects of the house.

Aside from the angled entrance area, interior planes are rigorously linear. Consequently, the free-form, freestanding fireplace is a startlingly sculptural element, as is the parapet of the stairway marked by abstract geometric cutouts. Like the fireplace in Breuer's Robinson house (1947), the Gagarin fireplace is positioned as an independent entity in the space, beyond which is an unbroken wall of windows open to the site. The fireplace becomes a sculptural piece and its solidity and presence are heightened by the glazed surfaces that frame it. The fireplace's two flues (one serves the fireplace in the children's living room below) branch off in sensuous curves. Constructing the tree-like fireplace required the meticulous construction of

On the north terrace,
a tree grows through
a large opening,
rimmed by sitting-
height fieldstone
walls and stainless
steel railings with
teak wood tops. The
northeast corner of
the living room at
right forms a rare
almost-glass corner,
though it includes a
structural column
encased in teak
wood.
photo: Ben Schnall

The sensuous, free-
form fireplace stands
alone in the living
room in front of a
small interior
greenhouse and a
wall of windows.
photo: Ben Schnall

wood forms that would contain the poured concrete. Its highly textured bush-hammered concrete is repeated on two walls of the interior greenhouse situated just behind the fireplace.

The exterior is a complex blend of materials, sun control devices, terraces, and solid and glass planes; while every elevation is varied, there is still a cohesiveness about the structure. Though the exterior is comprised of only four materials—local fieldstone, painted brick, painted board and batten, and glass—it is in the way they are configured and treated on each facade that an overall complexity results.

It is a virtual axiom of Breuer and Beckhard houses that planes remain pure, either all glass or solid forms—though here there is a rare glass corner of sorts in the living room (a principal teak-encased column separates the two glass walls). The emphasis of this house and others is on the juxtaposition of glass and solid wall and where they meet. To carry a material around a corner is a Breuer and Beckhard rarity, especially at this time in their careers. If there were any rules or inclinations to their work, it was to have materials meet at corners and contrast rather than carry around.

Additional planes based on structural necessity are created at the terrace areas to the north. Exterior areas become outdoor rooms in a sense as a result of wood wall planes that resemble the structural framing sections of a house under construction. Instead of posts or solid walls supporting roof extensions, the open stud walls are functional forms as well as suggestive ones. By nature of their transparency, these walls define and contain space, making the interplay between interior and exterior living spaces among the most pronounced of all Breuer and Beckhard houses.

Both front and rear facades, as well as that facing the road, are marked by sun shading overhangs; on sunny days the shadows cast change the facades throughout the day. On the far right side of the entrance facade, for instance, solid sun shading is provided over windows while over solid walls open-form wood members are placed perpendicular to the line of the house, the idea being to maintain the benefit of the overhang where it is needed while also continuing the line of the roof. The alternating portions of solid overhangs, cutouts and the shadows cast are about as close to decorative effect as Breuer and Beckhard ever get.

Another terrace directly off the living and dining area, covered in bluestone (actually the roof of

the lower level), overlooks a swimming pool and the rolling hills of the countryside. A tree that was specifically planted grows through a large cutout. Fieldstone walls and open railings with elegant teak wood caps trace portions of the terraces, while tall and vigorously articulated fieldstone walls at grade level eventually burrow into the ground. A stairway, with its riserless treads cantilevered from the fieldstone wall, leads to the pool area. These bold stairs and the minimalist sculptural railings reveal Breuer's early prowess as a furniture designer. The stairway is a kind of Breuer standard and is found at many of the houses. A wall to the south of the pool pro-

vides privacy from the street. In 1958, the sculptor Costantino Nivola created a true graffiti work on both sides of the wall that recounts the history of the Gagarin family. The technique involved covering the brick with a layer of dark plaster. After it had dried a white plaster was then applied; while still wet shapes and forms were cut into it to reveal the dark plaster beneath. Color was then applied much like a fresco technique.

That a house this large and long could remain modest is an attribute. In terms of layout the house is comprised, ultimately, of two rectangles connected by courtyards and terraces. On the outside

the house appears to be among the most complicated. Yet the house is able to tolerate that complexity because the materials have homogeneity and each in themselves is restrained. While the relationship among the materials is complex, the relationships and overall form are handled skillfully. Despite all of the various elements there is a clearly articulated desire for simplicity and compatibility.

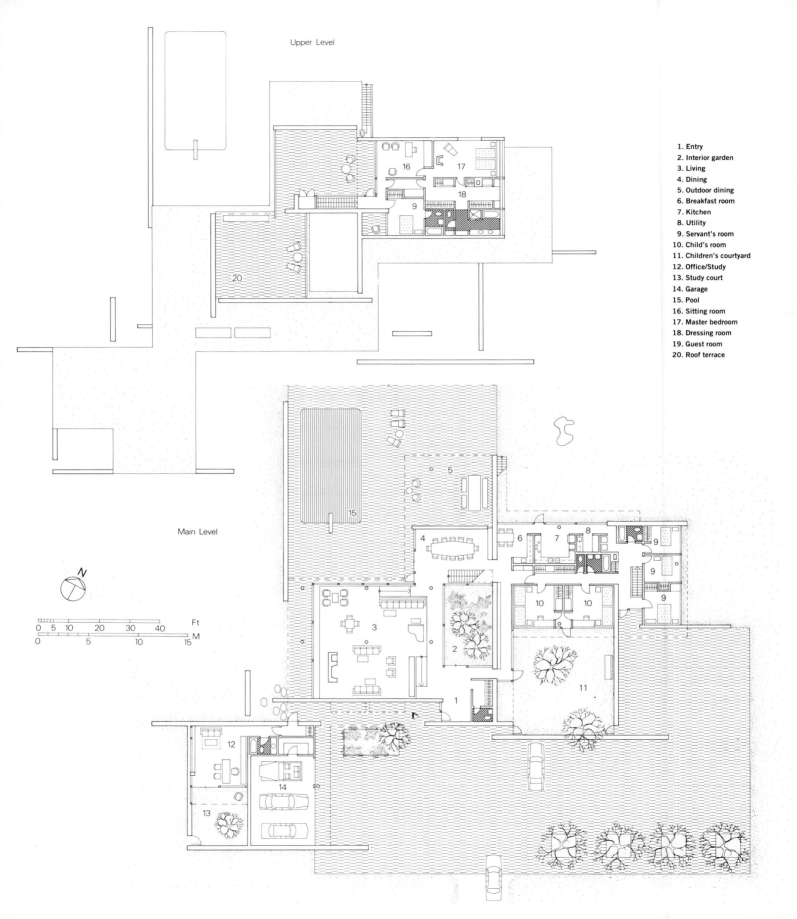

Upper Level

Main Level

1. Entry
2. Interior garden
3. Living
4. Dining
5. Outdoor dining
6. Breakfast room
7. Kitchen
8. Utility
9. Servant's room
10. Child's room
11. Children's courtyard
12. Office/Study
13. Study court
14. Garage
15. Pool
16. Sitting room
17. Master bedroom
18. Dressing room
19. Guest room
20. Roof terrace

N

0 5 10 20 30 40 Ft
0 5 10 15 M

Zurich, Switzerland, 1957
Approximately 9,000 square feet
Marcel Breuer, Architect/Herbert Beckhard, Associate
Eberhard Eidenbenz, Associate in Switzerland

At the south elevation the entrance appears hidden, a frequent Breuer and Beckhard device. From this approach the house appears as a series of parallel planes, comprised of either stucco or stone. Shadows are cast by cutouts in the roof.
photo: Bernhard Moosbrugger

Glass walls and solid forms, horizontal planes and vertical elements, balance and asymmetry, traditional cobblestone paving and frank concrete surfacing, a sharply geometric swimming pool and formal landscaping against wooded hills and an expansive body of water—such deliberate and conspicuous contradictions make the Staehelin house unpredictable from its various vantage points. Each view presents a different house. And a free-flowing, informal plan within makes for interiors that are varied, evocative, and surprising. The three-acre site, uncommonly large for Zurich, with its views of the Zurich See and nearby woods, and the client's wishes for

a large home allowed Breuer and Beckhard to indulge in materials, volumes, and highly articulated facades—but not so much that the structure "become[s] complicated and full of details" cautioned Breuer in a 1962 interview about the house in *Interiors* magazine.

When Breuer and Beckhard designed the Staehelin house in the mid-1950s, it was an especially productive time for the firm in Europe. Breuer was working, in collaboration with Bernard Zehrfuss and Pier Luigi Nervi, on the UNESCO project in Paris, the De Bijenkorf Department Store in Rotterdam, the U.S. Embassy in the Hague, and an office building in Amsterdam. During these fre-

quent trips to Europe, Breuer established many client contacts, of whom Bill (Willy) and Mariana Staehelin was one (another important residential commission was the Koerfer house on Lago Maggiore, Switzerland). Among aficionados of Modern architecture, like Staehelin, Breuer was well known in Zurich. His Doldertal Apartments of 1935, which he designed in collaboration with Alfred and Emil Roth, were lauded for their house-like feel and configuration, amply fenestrated walls, and exposed columns. Indeed, those exposed columns and the way the stucco surfaces were rendered are echoed here. The apartments remain important fixtures in Zurich.

From the entry approach to the Staehelin house, two of the three principal wall surface materials—stone and stucco—are apparent. Here the house appears to have uncompromised solidity. Yet, once inside, the house's open quality is revealed; the solid form is opened up considerably with courtyards and terraces and a vertical element containing two bedrooms. Unlike in America where stucco is still the exception for houses, in Europe—and Switzerland especially—it is an indigenous material. Breuer and Beckhard gave the stucco wall at the notched entrance to the house a special prominence by inserting openings in the overhang so that at certain times of day the walls are marked by ever-changing rectangular blocks of sunlight—a

The west elevation is essentially the principal view of the house. A relatively high-ceilinged ground level is topped by an upper level containing master bedroom and guest room. The stone wall at right is the independent studio wing.
photo: Bernhard Moosbrugger

On the north elevation an oversize window marks the master bedroom. An exterior staircase leads from the upper terrace to grade level.
photo: Bernhard Moosbrugger

fleeting decorative element. While stone is the chief component of the front or south elevation of the house, there are hints of glass walls beyond, peeking up just above the six-foot six-inch-high stone walls. The entry approach, devoid of openings in order to maintain privacy from the road—except for a lone window-like cutout in the stone wall at the entrance—is an inviting one nonetheless, a result in part of the traditional European fishtail granite paving of the driveway. Also, the several stone walls, of varying height and set on different parallel planes, beckon as they speak of an expansive house with multiple living spaces and various treatments.

From most views the sprawling house appears to be one story, but the master bedroom suite and guest bedroom are situated on a second floor. Though the ample site could easily have accommodated a one-story house, there was an advantage to getting up in the air and capturing the views. Also, the second floor created the kind of asymmetrical dynamics that the architects so often favor; the second floor element makes for contrasting volumes. Despite the elevated portion, though, the house remains a decidedly earthbound structure.

The second floor includes a terrace that is larger in size than the space within. And like the other zones of the house—the first floor living areas, the kitchen and bedrooms, and a studio situated in

a separate wing with its own private court—the upstairs has its own entrance reached by an exterior flight of stairs with open risers leading directly to the swimming pool and garden. There is also an interior stairway placed intriguingly against a window wall of the interior courtyard.

The living room is sunk 18 inches, and is reached from one of two short ramps. Consequently, unlike elsewhere in the house, the windowsill, instead of being at floor level, is raised. For the client, an avid art collector (there are eight Henry Moores on the property), the windowsill acts not only as a continuous window seat but as an ideal base for displaying sculpture.

The main living spaces focus on an intimate interior garden. The garden captures space and provides a contrasting experience to simply looking out a window, while also visually extending the boundaries of the room. A freestanding bush-hammered concrete fireplace is another visual anchor for the space. Two children's bedrooms

A detail of the
west facade
photo: Bernhard
Moosbrugger.

At once, all
of the building's
materials become
visible at the entry—
cobblestones, stuc-
co, rough stone,
and board form
concrete soffits.
photo: Bernhard
Moosbrugger

face a large courtyard, sized for
play. The client, an attorney, was
especially concerned with the
safety of his children and requested that the architects situate their
bedrooms well within the house.
The courtyard onto which those
bedrooms face provides an additional safety buffer; so the space
acts as both a private domain and
a secure one.

While the living and dining
areas embrace views of both the

small interior garden and the
Zurich See, overt views of the
swimming pool are deliberately
minimized. Whenever Breuer and
Beckhard design swimming pools
they make it a point to have them
close by but out of the primary
view. Beckhard especially objects
to a pool being a conspicuous
feature. Simply put, a pool de-
serves its own setting, especially in
winter when a covered pool is not
an appealing sight.

Ceilings within, as well as
roof overhangs and the underside
of the covering soffits at exterior
living areas, are of poured concrete. They were cast in carefully
built wood board molds, and the
imprint of those boards is visible.
Equally vigorous are the floors,
which are made of random-sized
split-face local granite slabs laid in
an offset pattern.

When conceiving the interior
plan, the architects decided on

chitects took advantage of it, the Staehelin house has an infinite quality about it. Every room, even those wholly within the envelope of the house, captures views and additional living spaces suggesting limitless boundaries. The house is not so much complicated as it is varied. Spaces created by roof overhangs, extended stone walls, courtyards, terraces, and stairways are many and each distinct. The sheer variety of expression apparent at each elevation creates a house that is uninhibited, and thus thoroughly Modern.

While not completely out of view, the swimming pool does not interfere with the principal view out to the Zurich See.
photo: Bernhard Moosbrugger

The interior stairway rises against a window wall of the interior garden. As a sort of archetype of the architects' staircases, stone slabs are supported on a metal rail. Because there are no risers, the staircase has a distinctly transparent quality.
photo: Bernhard Moosbrugger

large expanses of space without walls. To do so, textually rich freestanding columns of bush-hammered concrete are revealed in the living room, dining area, kitchen, one of the children's rooms, and a servant's room, resulting in a pavilion-like expanse. The columns act as important elements that articulate the structure and form of the house. The neutral colors of the materials—light gray concrete, dark granite, bluish-gray ashlar set stone, white stucco—allow for great freedom in furnishings. The house is able, in fact, to accommodate furnishings as diverse as Louis XIV chairs set at a gray granite slab dining table designed by the architects.

Despite the house's great size, it is, ultimately, a modest and restrained composition. Materials are basic and indigenous, colors muted, and spaces scaled for a family. Yet, by virtue of its setting and the manner in which the ar-

From the dining
room there is an
inspiring view of
the Zurich See.
Louis XIV chairs
complement a
Breuer and
Beckhard-designed
granite dining
table.
photo: Bernhard
Moosbrugger

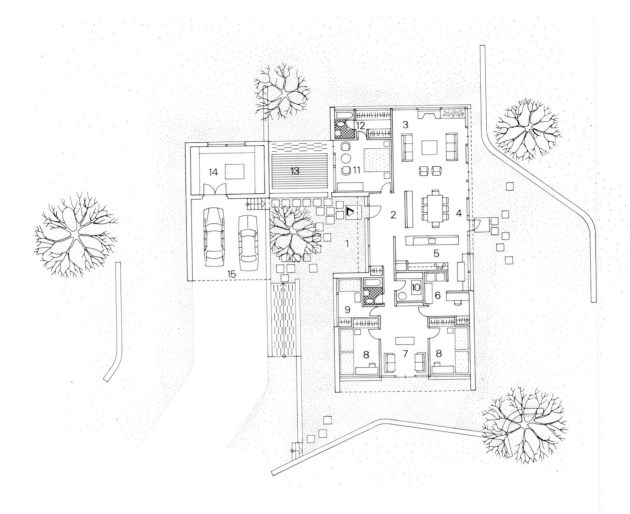

1. Entry court
2. Entry
3. Living
4. Dining
5. Kitchen
6. Utility
7. Children's living room
8. Child's bedroom
9. Maid's room
10. Mechanical
11. Master bedroom
12. Dressing room
13. Pond
14. Shop/Storage
15. Carport

N

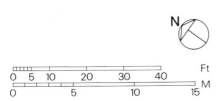

Ft
0 5 10   20   30   40

M
0   5   10   15

Laaff
House

Andover, Massachusetts, 1957
Approximately 3,200 square feet
Marcel Breuer, Architect/Herbert Beckhard, Associate

The entrance ramp, designed in collaboration with landscape architect Dan Kiley, is a mix of cobblestones, grassy patches, and rectangular granite stones, edged by two low fieldstone walls. The ramp leads into an inviting, grassy courtyard entrance area.
photo: Ben Schnall

Glass and stone, and their inherently opposing natures, is a much-exploited dynamic in Breuer and Beckhard houses. That conflict or plot of sorts becomes even more compelling and unpredictable in the Laaff House, where stone contrasts with stone while glass also has a strong role in otherwise largely solid walls.

Many of the Breuer and Beckhard stone and/or stucco and glass houses keep planes largely pure—either solely glazed or solid. At the Laaff house, unlike any of their other houses, most of the fieldstone walls have been whitewashed while a few are left natural, with walls on the same facade often having both treatments; in addition, some of these same planes contain windows. Referring to the Laaff house in an interview with *Architectural Record* when it was named a "Record House" for 1960, Breuer said that "the real impact of any work is the extent to which it unifies contrasting notions . . . . *I mean unifies and not compromises.*" So while the individual characteristics of natural-colored fieldstone, whitewashed stone, and glass remain keen, the way they interact on the building makes for a complete and unique story.

The whitewashing of stone was anticipated from the moment Breuer and Beckhard conceived the design for the house. According to Beckhard, the notion to whitewash the stone was inspired by an affection for Greek and Italian houses in the Mediterranean and Adriatic regions where stone is frequently painted white. By whitewashing stone, mortar joints achieve a different relationship to the stone; the very difference in color between the stones and mortar joints is eliminated. What results is not individual stones traced by joints but a consistently potent and rugged singular texture. In collaborative and on individual projects Breuer and Beckhard had whitewashed and painted brick or concrete block—the Pack house addition, the Kacmarcik house, the Gagarin house, the Sarah Lawrence College Arts Center, the Ferry House dormitory at Vassar—but never stone. The whitewashing of the Laaff house is not, however, a complete one. Generally, high (eight foot) stone walls are painted while lower ones below windows and in the garden are left natural.

Convincing the clients, George and Marian Laaff, of the aesthetic merit of whitewashing the stone was a bit of a challenge. Beckhard recalls that when all the walls were in place, Mr. Laaff made a last-minute pitch to avoid having them painted. Breuer and Beckhard convinced him after a number of discussions that it was a key conceptual idea and essential to the design. Ultimately, the architects prevailed and Mr. Laaff was pleased when the project was complete.

In keeping with the Mediterranean strain and the subsequent

images the house evokes of centuries-old building traditions, landscape architect Dan Kiley—in the first of a number of projects in which Breuer and Beckhard worked with him—further developed the entrance court and ramp that gives the house a kind of ritualized approach. The wide, gently sloped ramp is edged by low fieldstone walls, while the surface is a mix of cobblestones, grassy patches, and strips of granite stones. This rising entry seems appropriate to the five-acre semi-suburban site with its grassy undulating topography. There is a ruinous, ancient quality to the approach, an aspect that Beckhard especially has fostered

in other houses, such as the guest quarters for the Bratti house and the dramatic porches and entry stair of the Schwartz house.

The ramp brings the visitor to the higher elevation of the house and a spacious courtyard entrance area. As a separate wing, the carport-storage facility remains at a slightly lower elevation. While Breuer's second New Canaan home was the inspiration for Mr. Laaff choosing the architects, he did ask for considerably more storage space, a woodworking shop, and a garage.

Aside from the strictly linear walls of the ramp and another screening wall that separates the master bedroom courtyard from

the one at the entry, retaining walls, garden walls, and others are essentially free flowing in form. They are treated as an element of the landscape, and so remain unpainted. The curving, sensuous forms of these walls contrast with the pure geometry of the house— all the time adhering to Breuer's requisite that no one element compromise another. Echoes of this idea are heard in a lecture Breuer gave at the University of Michigan in 1963: "We are in the flow of transition from . . . transparent architecture to one which sets solid elements next to transparency, and a new plasticity next to lineal purity. An architecture unifying vivid contrasts and demonstrating a much broader vocabulary."

Upon passing through the somewhat formalized exterior entry court, one enters an interior entryway that is spacious and allows the visitor to pause before entering rooms. The organization of the house plan has similarities to Breuer's second New Canaan home. Access to the master bedroom area is immediate, quickly defining the adult wing as being separate from the children's; a hallway connects these two distinct zones. Horizontal bands of windows whose sills are at eye level mark both the entry area and the wall behind the fireplace in the living area. This treatment makes for different kinds of views and continues the line of the fireplace wall. Breuer built a similar wall in his second New

At left, part of one
of the free-flowing
fieldstone walls on
the south facade
that contrast with
the more linear
geometry of the
house. Sliding full-
height glass doors
lead from the dining
and living areas to
the outdoors.
photo: Ben Schnall

A view from the living area toward the dining area. A floor-to-ceiling bookcase shields the dining area from the entrance. The kitchen is situated behind a low sink unit and is essentially included in the living/dining space.
photo: Ben Schnall

Canaan home. In addition to lessening the solidity of these walls, the windows, almost clerestory in function and placement, bring in light while maintaining privacy.

Once inside there is easy access to the open living/dining area and minimally separated kitchen. The children's bedrooms and guest bedroom are clustered around a central playroom/family room, through which one circulates to get to the bedrooms. The master bedroom with its expansive glass areas is given a high degree of privacy with its own courtyard. With the architects, Kiley fashioned a small fish pond and an area for outdoor dining in

the bedroom courtyard, which remains open to the site on one side.

Breuer and Beckhard's interest in the way texture is created by white painted stone carries to the interior. The major living room wall in which the stone fireplace is situated is whitewashed, treated just as if it was an exterior wall. Deep-red clay tile flooring throughout the interior is laid with small joints, contrary to the way such flooring is usually configured. To do so, the architects used true accurate sides and offset joints. Strong contrasts between the deep-red floor and the otherwise white walls—painted stone or gypsum board—and honey-colored

cedar ceilings make for animated interiors and help foster the sense of dichotomy that is important to the house as a whole.

While every Breuer and Beckhard house incorporates the key design features for which the architects are known, here each element—material, window, structural element—has a keen prominence. What happens to stone when it is whitewashed is made all the more real by those sections of wall where stone is left natural. Indeed, Breuer insisted, as he once said of his Gane Pavilion, that "when stone is used in a wall, the aim is not to evoke some notion of rock, but to build a clear-cut slab. . . . It should be clear that this is a wall built by a mason . . . not a grotto. . . ." The function of the windows for introducing light versus those for circulation and views are described respectively by the clerestory windows in the living area and the floor-length ones in the bedrooms. The interior plan is informal and open, and free-flowing walls on the site echo this arrangement. Yet the entrance ramp imbues the house with a degree of formality; walls in the courtyard of the master bedroom privatize and contain the space, though the lack of a fourth wall establishes a sense of freedom. In such opposition there is great individual expression and ultimate unity.

The band of glass
above the fireplace
wall brings in morn-
ing light. Deep-red
clay tile flooring
highlights the
whitewashed walls
and cedar ceilings.
photo: Ben Schnall

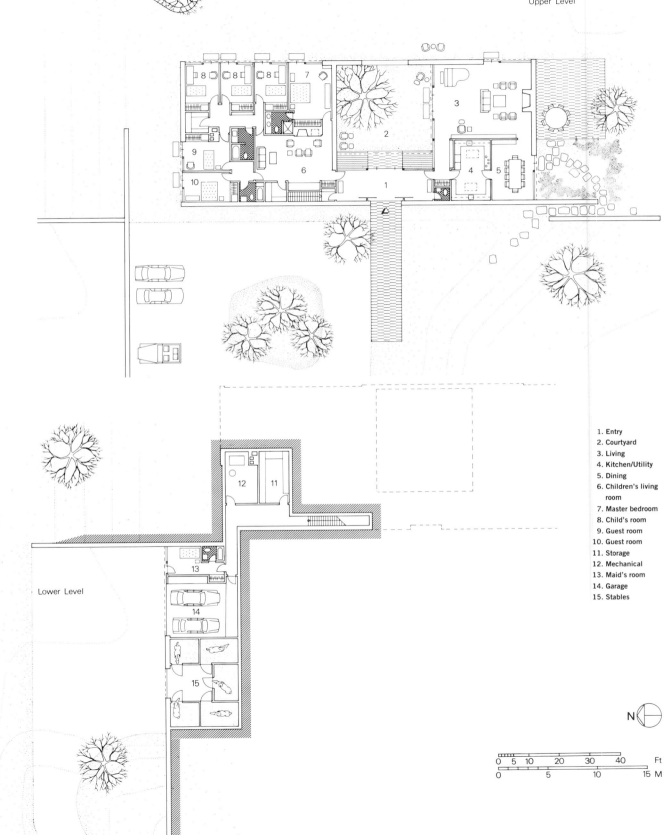

Upper Level

1. Entry
2. Courtyard
3. Living
4. Kitchen/Utility
5. Dining
6. Children's living room
7. Master bedroom
8. Child's room
9. Guest room
10. Guest room
11. Storage
12. Mechanical
13. Maid's room
14. Garage
15. Stables

Lower Level

N

0 5 10   20   30   40   Ft
0   5   10   15 M

Hooper House

Baltimore County, Maryland, 1960
Approximately 7,800 square feet
Marcel Breuer, Architect/Herbert Beckhard, Associate

From the driveway the full sweep of the west-facing stone wall—140 feet long—that defines the entrance elevation comes into view. The glass doors, behind which is a glass wall to the courtyard, gives the otherwise solid house a sense of transparency.
photo: Ben Schnall

"Mother and Breuer worked extremely well together; they spoke the same language," says Jay Williams, one of the three daughters of the clients, Arthur and Edith Hooper. Much of that language translated as understatement, simplicity, boldness, abstraction.

Mrs. Hooper had a strong attraction to Modern design. As a young woman she had worked in the design department of the Museum of Modern Art in New York where, according to her daughter, "she fell in love with contemporary architecture." Her brother, W. Hawkins Ferry, was an architect who lived in a Modern house he had designed in Grosse

Pointe, Michigan; her father, Dexter Ferry, had commissioned Breuer (at the urging of Edith) in 1950 to design a dormitory at Vassar College, the Ferry House. The small, almost domestically scaled cooperative dormitory for 26 students was noted for its pronounced separation of communal and dormitory rooms; each room was in turn characterized by distinct study and sleeping zones. Prior to the completion of this house in 1960, the Hoopers had been clients of Breuer on another house. The couple and their three daughters had been living in a traditional Georgian style house (which Mr. Hooper had built) in Baltimore to which Breuer had

added a highly Modern three-bedroom addition in 1948. Effectively combining such diverse styles was no easy feat, and at the time the new wing received considerable publicity.

The Hoopers had acquired a seven-acre site in suburban Baltimore and Mrs. Hooper—the active client as opposed to her husband—was intent on erecting on it a thoroughly Modern house. Mrs. Hooper had shown enthusiasm for an Eliot Noyes house she had seen in New Canaan, Connecticut. The house by Noyes, who was a friend and former student of Breuer's, was distinguished by two wings separated by a large courtyard. "She loved the Eliot Noyes house but didn't like the fact that you had to go outside to enter each of the house's compartments," says Mrs. Williams. Here the same idea of a courtyard linking separate wings exists but with considerable modification. Mrs. Hooper's careful attention to the design of the house applied also to the sculpture, paintings, and furnishings, combined with many built-in furniture pieces designed by the architects.

From the entrance side, the house appears as a long (140 feet) stone wall interrupted only by a doorway cut into it at its midpoint. The entire sweep of the facade is visible, and the vibrant rusts and grays of the Maryland fieldstone that comprise it are intrinsically decorative. In that sense this principal material, let alone the architecture it determines, cannot be

Visible at the rear is the cutout in the east courtyard wall and the bedroom wing, marked by its glass wall. Sliding floor-to-ceiling glass doors from every bedroom allow easy access to the outdoors.
photo: Walter Smalling

A view through the cutout into the landscaped courtyard. When the sliding glass entrance doors and those beyond are open, one can walk right through the house; doors also lead directly from the living/dining area to the outside.
photo: Walter Smalling

ignored by the visitor. It is a material few have seen on so large a scale and erected in such a fashion. Given that it is such a formidable wall, it made sense to use a fieldstone that was imbued with strong colors. This is a prime example of the notion that the material itself satisfies the need for surface interest—thus decoration without decoration.

At a certain crucial point at the approach, the transparent quality of the house can be seen. Behind the wide entryway, with its two sliding glass doors, is a large courtyard at the end of which is another stone wall with a large opening. As a result, one can look literally through the house. And if both the front doors and the sliding glass door onto the courtyard are left open, one can walk right through the house. While the front facade is a solid form, the rear one is chiefly glazed.

By their deliberate asymmetrical placement, major elements compete for attention. The large glass entrance doors at first appear centered in the stone wall, but the fact that the wall on the right extends beyond the edge of the house returns the entrance into an asymmetrical mode. A huge oak tree in the courtyard that rises high above the house—and off-center from the entrance doors—is a startling vertical element in an otherwise horizontal building. The rectangular cutout in the rear wall of the courtyard is also not centered.

The courtyard separates the

living from the sleeping wing with an enclosed walkway linking the two areas; in fact, the courtyard is flanked by what is essentially two buildings. The spacious living room has views through floor-to-ceiling windows onto both the courtyard and out to Robert E. Lee Park and Lake Roland. The dining room, shielded from the courtyard, has another full-height window (as are all the windows in the house) that looks out onto a grassy area and trees beyond. As a way to maximize precious wall space and to create a different lighting sensation, the kitchen, and the family/children's room in the other wing, are lit only by skylights. As a result of the overhead natural light that fills the space, these two interior rooms have a slightly exterior feel to them. Though it would have been an easy matter for the architects to cut a window in the outside wall of the kitchen, the idea was to contain the two rooms at the front of the house and to let the house open up beyond them.

The family/children's room acts as the focal point for six bedrooms. Because this space is lit by skylights, the quality of light that characterizes it is very different from those in the bedrooms, each of which is distinguished by an entire wall of windows. In the master bedroom and another bedroom, the Maryland fieldstone is brought inside. Certain walls in the living and dining areas are also stone. Bush-hammered concrete fireplaces, simpler in form than others of the architects, are in both

A simple but impos-
ing bush-hammered
concrete fireplace is
compatible with, yet
a strong contrast to,
the large slabs of
bluestone flooring
and the multi-hued
fieldstone wall. The
living area looks out
onto Lake Roland
and the park beyond.
photo: Walter Smalling

As in the living and dining areas, the Maryland fieldstone has been brought inside one of the bedrooms. To save space in the relatively small bedrooms, major furniture units are built-in.
photo: Ben Schnall

The dining area has a view and access to its own grassy courtyard. Stone has been brought inside to most of the living and dining area walls.
photo: Walter Smalling

the living and the family rooms, each marked by the trademark Breuer and Beckhard bluestone flooring.

Despite the open plan, the house maintains privacy among its parts. The solid north wall of the courtyard shields the bedroom wing and its family/children's room from the living area. A service stairway to the partially below-grade garage, with its horse stables and maid's room, opens to the interior hallway. And of course the solid facade ensures that virtually no interior activity can be seen from the road. The courtyard was intended by Breuer and Beckhard to be a useful outdoor space, ideal for warm weather parties since it provides, simultaneously, sunny and shaded spots. Plantings include dwarf azaleas, ivy, ferns, and wisteria, and a fish pond running the length of the entry with a large bluestone slab bridge is situated just behind the sliding glass doors off the interior walk-way. The entire glass wall at the east side of the courtyard is covered by an overhang for sun and rain protection. Landscape architect Dan Kiley, who had first worked with Breuer and Beckhard on the Laaff house, was respon-sible in consort with the architects for the courtyard, entry approach, and other landscaping.

At the threshold of the main entrance, in the cutout of the courtyard rear wall, and at corners of the house where glass and solid planes intersect, the thickness of the stone walls is apparent.

Beckhard explains that he and Breuer made such walls 16 inches thick in order to fully reveal the inherent beauty of the stone. Also, they felt it necessary to emphasize thickness in order to correctly "work" the stone and articulate its mass. A low, curving stone wall following the grade at the rear of the house that acts as a tree well is a striking foil to the strict linear geometry of the house.

Beckhard who at the time was a young associate in Breuer's firm responsible among other things for the on-site supervision of the house, remembers that despite the vastness of the house, there were relatively few construction draw-ings needed for it as compared to most of the houses they had done. Considering that the house re-quired not much more than two wall sections to be drawn, it is about as straightforward as a building can get, both aesthetically and technically. So, in many ways the house is not only simple in appearance but simple to build. By virtue of its simplicity, the house is assertive and yet has great repose and stability. The house stands on its own and there was no effort made to embellish it. Indeed, the only relieving element is the landscape.

A view along the
corridor leading from
the entry area that
connects living and
sleeping zones. Large
bluestone slabs, at
right, serve as a
bridge over a fish
pond in the court-
yard, which is ac-
cessible from the
entry area.
photo: Walter Smalling

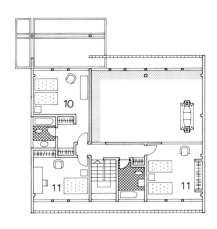

Upper Level

1. Entry
2. Maid's room
3. Mechanical
4. Garage
5. Living
6. Study
7. Dining
8. Kitchen
9. Utility
10. Master bedroom
11. Child's bedroom

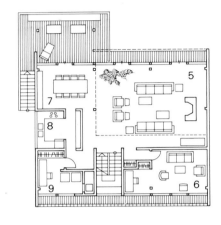

Main Level

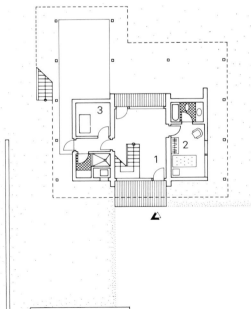

Lower Level

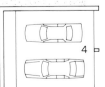

N

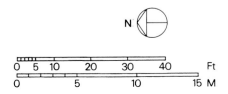

0 5 10   20   30   40   Ft
0   5   10   15 M

McMullen House

Mantoloking, New Jersey, 1960
Approximately 4,400 square feet
Marcel Breuer, Architect/Herbert Beckhard, Associate

The entrance facade or west side with its full sun screen. The pedestal upon which the house rests is essentially solid, except for a glazed portion through which one can look to the ocean at the back.
photo: Ben Schnall

In deciding upon Breuer and Beckhard as architects for their vacation house on the New Jersey shore, Jacquie McMullen remembers thinking that "if you're going to build today, build what's going on today. Find the best contemporary architect working and go with that. Breuer was very interesting to work with and I have to admit I stood in awe of the man. We weren't wholly removed from the design process but Breuer and Beckhard pretty much got their way."

Mantoloking is typical of the New Jersey shore towns. A virtually uninterrupted line of dwellings set on narrow lots marks the coastline. Breuer and Beckhard had to fash-ion a house that maintained privacy from the busy roadway and from adjacent neighbors to the north and south, as well as open up as much as possible to the expansive beach and ocean at the rear. Their solution called for what is essentially a two-story rectangular block with solid sides raised above a smaller one-story base. By elevating the house, views were maximized, potential storm damage was avoided, and an ocean breeze was more easily captured. Also, by defining the house as an elevated element, Breuer and Beckhard were able to reveal the house's structure; their ideal of exploiting the technical is as visible here as in any of their houses. The structural system is very much exposed and emphasized as an aesthetic element.

The elevated portion of the entrance or west facade is a vast expanse of glass protected by a fixed louvered sun screen stained a brown/black color. The structure manages to both provide protection from the sun and maintain privacy from the roadway. All of the support posts (both inside and outside), exterior railings, and sun screens are stained dark. Against the otherwise white house, such technical features are distinct. At the ground floor entry a floor-to-ceiling rectangular window next to the door allows the visitor to look through the house to the ocean at the back. The bold two-story cube that hovers over this understated, semi-transparent ground level is cantilevered five feet on all four sides from a base of glass and concrete block. A system of conspicuous, heavy wood columns and beams supports the house. Two-inch-diameter galvanized steel pins emerge from the bottoms of the posts, similar to those at the Starkey house. A U-shaped steel bracket is bolted to each column, and the resulting pin is sunk into a concrete foundation. The pins and bolts are exposed not for mere bravado—though their effect is compelling—but as a way to prevent rotting of the wood by isolating it from the ground. The purely technical consideration becomes an aesthetic element as well.

The south and north sides of the house are of board and batten

The east side beach
elevation. The trans-
parent quality of the
house is revealed
through the first floor
window wall. The
house and its decks
are connected to the
ground through
regularly spaced posts
which are held off the
ground by stainless
steel pins. The sun
shade of the entry side
is used only at the
upper portion of the
main living space.
photo: Ben Schnall

The configuration of free beams over the deck suggests a roof surface and in so doing captures and defines outdoor space. Dark stained wood contrasts with the white board and batten siding of the house.
photo: Ben Schnall

painted off-white. Except for two narrow horizontal sliding windows cut into the north side, the walls are solid because of the proximity of neighboring dwellings. The rear of the house is a near duplicate of the front, though only a portion of the glass facade—two-thirds of the top floor—is covered by a sun screen identical to that on the entry side. At the back it is especially apparent that the glass walls of the house are recessed three and a half feet from the sun screen. Breuer and Beckhard's notion of the way solid planes should intersect with glass ones is expressed emphatically here. Where such contrasting planes meet, Breuer and Beckhard rarely

allow them to form flush corners in any of their houses. To emphasize these intersecting planes, independent fieldstone walls, extended roof lines, and other design features extend the planes beyond the envelopes of their houses, and in so doing capture and create additional outdoor spaces. While this house may appear to be a neat rectangle, the recesses allow Breuer and Beckhard to exercise their penchant for extending wall planes beyond their actual function of containing and defining the boundaries of interior space.

A further demonstration in cantilevered structures occurs with a deck off the dining area on the ocean side; the deck surface ex-

tends beyond the posts and beams that support it. A series of overhead beams suggests a frame or roof-like surface above the deck. For Beckhard those beams are an abstraction that captures space. As an articulation of space that is neither fully outside nor fully inside, the Breuer/Beckhard interest in melding interior with exterior spaces is reflected by the deck. Within the recess of the glass curtain wall is a balcony that leads into the deck. A staircase from the deck provides direct access down to the beach.

Apart from these floating elements there are more earthbound units on the site as well. A detached garage sits firmly on the ground at a right angle to the house. One garage door is painted Breuer-blue and the other Breuer-red, a shade that is esentially vermilion red. Against the dark/light house and the muted beach landscape, the garage doors are piercing splashes of color. There is also a Breuer-red side door on the first floor of the north facade. Two gray-painted concrete-block screening walls situated on the north and south sides define the edges of the property.

The small first level contains an entrance area, covered with bluestone flagging, in which an open staircase is placed, a maid's room and bath, as well as a utility room and a shower facility for those coming in from the beach. The second floor, or main living floor, is comprised of a monumental two-story-high living area, bor-

dered on two sides by the house's other rooms—dining room, kitchen, study, and laundry room on one level (a configuration not dissimilar to the much later Vasiliou house). Three bedrooms and two bathrooms are on the top floor.

Aside from its sheer height, the living room is remarkable for two details in particular. The sun screen that hangs from the top floor provides a more secretive, almost intimate view of the ocean than from the open expanses of glass. On sunny days, shadows created by the louvers play across the floor.

The other important detail is the bush-hammered concrete fire-place, which appears to be two inverted V's. In fact, Mrs. McMullen remembers the architects showing her the drawing for the fireplace: "I said that's terrific, but then it was pointed out that I had it upside down." To accommodate such a large opening, a double flue was needed. It is a particularly noteworthy exercise of how the architects make fireplaces sculptural elements even though they are decidedly functional elements. (Though more rigidly geometric, the McMullen fireplace echoes the exuberant form of the earlier Gagarin house fireplace.) The fireplace is further set off by its placement against a wall that is perhaps the largest expanse of

Breuer-blue in any of the houses.

The house could easily be likened to a traditional Japanese residential dwelling. The post-and-beam construction is brought to the interior and those members are stained dark. Like Japanese interiors, they contrast with natural wood trim and white plaster walls. Four Japanese lanterns, the principal lighting source, hang in the living area, and sisal matting, not unlike Japanese tatami, is used as a floor covering. The dark wood moldings in each room are one of the strongest interior features; the moldings frame each room, not unlike the way the beams above the outside deck frame that space. Even the soffit board above the garage doors is a dark stained wood member that neatly edges the structure. This interplay of moldings, posts, and bare white walls is one example for Mrs. McMullen of how "the house has a sense of detail that a lot of modern houses don't have."

Given the long line of undistinguished traditional beach houses that line the Mantoloking shore, the McMullen house is a startling vision. Yet, despite its departure in design from its generic neighbors, the McMullen house manages to be compatible, for what it really does, more so perhaps than the other houses on the beach, is acknowledge and fulfill its role as a modest ocean-front dwelling. By doing so it serves as a Modern example of what a vacation house can be.

As in many of Breuer
and Beckhard houses,
sisal matting is used
instead of carpeting.
The highly sculptural
bush-hammered
concrete fireplace
with its two flues is
the centerpiece of the
living/dining area.
The two flues are
necessary because of
the large opening of
the fireplace.
photo: Ben Schnall

1. **Entry/Bridge**
2. **Living/Dining**
3. **Kitchen**
4. **Porch**
5. **Child's bedroom**
6. **Master bedroom**
7. **Guest bedroom/**
   Studio

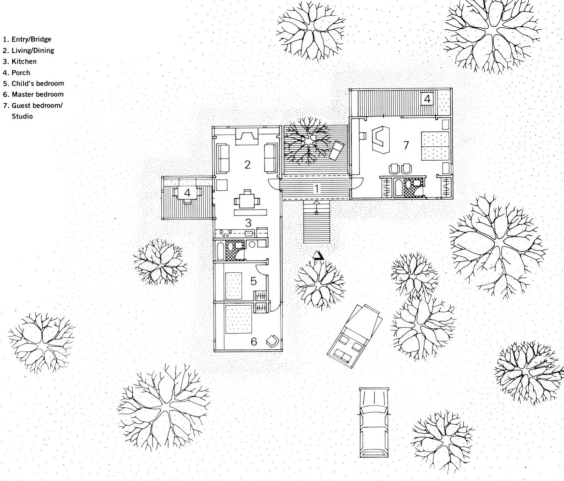

N

Ft
0 5 10   20   30   40

M
0   5   10   15

Wise House

Wellfleet, Massachusetts, 1963
Approximately 1,600 square feet
Marcel Breuer and Herbert Beckhard, Architects

The studio wing (at right) remains wholly independent yet readily accessible to the main wing of the house. The frameless, horizontal sliding windows, a Breuer-invented system, were first used by Breuer on his own Wellfleet house. Trees are typical Cape Cod scrub pines.
photo: Joseph W. Molitor

Aside from large-scale developments or low-income housing solutions, serious, creative architects are often uneasy about building a particular house more than once. Clearly, issues of professional ethics, integrity, and fees charged come into play; but there is also the aspect of the architect as artist whereby each built creation is its own separate act. Aside from differing site constraints and client needs that determine a house's layout and function, there is something troubling for an architect about repeating a uniquely articulated aesthetic ideal. For a client who wanted a duplicate version of his own home, Beckhard recalls that he felt compelled to do

something unique, in part because of the urge to always improve upon a finished product. He finds it difficult to believe that any creative endeavor is ever truly finished. To clone a house would be to go against the urge to refine.

When Howard Wise, a prominent New York art dealer, first saw the house Breuer had built for himself in 1948 in the Cape Cod town of Wellfleet, he felt that it perfectly articulated his wishes for a summer retreat—a modest, rustic, attractive, adaptable house. When he commissioned Breuer and Beckhard in 1963 for a house that was to be built in the same town, he made it clear that he wanted Breuer's house identically.

Furthermore, the sites were virtually identical—hilly, sandy terrain interspersed with scrubby pitch pines. Aside from a reversed floor plan as a result of the way the house was to be positioned on the site, the Wise house is a virtual mirror image of Breuer's—at least in the final form that Breuer's house took. (Fortunately, the houses were far enough away from each other in town to keep them distinct entities.)

Only partly for economic reasons, Breuer's house when completed was almost primitive in terms of domestic comforts. The rectangular house was sheathed in a thin layer of plywood that, while covered by vertical cedar boards on the exterior, remained untouched on the inside of the house. There were no interior finishes; studs and joists in raw states were fully visible for years until Breuer decided to do some refining. Beckhard has said that "Breuer liked that rough, unfinished look. It hearkens, in fact, to the larger issue of polished architecture versus a basic, almost rough version. We've never aimed at polishing buildings, but to keep things instead as much as possible in a natural, spontaneous, found state. There's something very basic, very primal about the architecture we've done, and Breuer's house exemplified that."

This summer retreat was not dissimilar from the first New Canaan house Breuer built for himself. Here as there, the house is a single, narrow, rectangular element with a circulation route along

The undulating
landscape has an
intimate relation-
ship to the house
as it is allowed to
flow beneath it.
Posts of varying
length are ground-
ed in individual
concrete foundations.
photo: Joseph W. Molitor

one side and all of the rooms facing the other side. Both houses are defined by their floating quality above the ground, and in each a dramatically cantilevered porch becomes an important outdoor living space.

In 1961, Breuer and Beckhard added to Breuer's house a separate studio for his son. The addition, which can function as a separate house with its own kitchenette, bathroom, and fireplace, is connected to the original house by an entry porch/breezeway. Though in essence another complete house, it is comprised of the same materials and details as the main house. Vertical cedar boarding is used on the exterior,

horizontal bands of sliding frameless windows mark the facades, and the same highly conspicuous structural system is employed. It was that completed version that was virtually wholly adapted for the Wise house. The horizontal window system is a Breuer invention, used here for the first time, and repeated in later houses. As with chairs, lamps, fireplaces, and an interest in using innovative materials, the windows exemplify Breuer's lifelong desire to devise new products. For Beckhard, too, standard products are not necessarily the only ones to be considered.

Among the most romantic characteristics of the Wise house

is the notion that the very landscape on which it is built be allowed to literally go through the house, a feat accomplished by a clearly expressed support system. The house is elevated above the sinuously flowing grade by means of heavy four-inch by four-inch posts of varying length. Each post is then supported by individual round concrete foundations. The contours of the earth remain visible and those undulating shapes become an integral part of the composition of the facades of the house.

Just as conspicuous as the house's supporting posts is the structure that allows the enclosed dining porch to be cantilevered over the site. Supported by a wood truss that is visible on the outside, its counterpoint supporting brace is visible within and becomes an active interior element. However, unlike other cantilevered porches, Breuer had this one and the one at his house screened. Though he would have preferred to have them open to the elements, even Breuer acknowledged that outdoor living had limits, especially when it came to the greenhead flies that menace Cape Cod in summers.

Interior finishes are simple but nonetheless cozy. In certain places, such as the bedroom portion of the studio and the seating area of the main house, the structure of the house is revealed by dark stained wood members; these members come to act as frames for the spaces. Interior wall surfaces are of Homasote, a ma-

terial made of compressed paper that comes in large sheets. (Breuer and Beckhard used the material again, though in a different form, in the ceiling of the Stillman II house.) Homasote is a very prosaic material and the architects were aware of its slightly crude quality, and even welcomed that look. Also, it is inexpensive, durable, and easy to install since the joints do not need to be taped the way they do with gypsum board. Ceilings are comprised of large subdivided plywood boards.

While settees in the living room are built-in pieces, the almost disarming simplicity of the living spaces make them adjust-able places as well. The house encourages people to live rather ruggedly and, in so doing, can accommodate a variety of furn-ishings. Indeed, the whole em-phasis of the house is one of informality.

The deck/breezeway that linked the main house with the studio in Breuer's home soon became an important gathering place, so much so that it functioned as a central outdoor living space. As a result, Breuer and Beckhard built an expanded version of it for Wise, which features a lower deck, through which pines grow, adjacent to the main deck/breezeway.

The spacious studio includes a fireplace and a deck of its own.
photo: Joseph W. Molitor

The living/dining area. Ceilings are of plywood, a material that fascinated Breuer as early as his student days at the Bauhaus. A familiar horizontal window is situated at the top of the fireplace box.
photo: Joseph W. Molitor

Both the Breuer and Wise houses reveal a profound respect for their sites. Neither terrain nor foliage was disturbed. The characteristics of the site become, in fact, integral features of the built composition. As growth occurs with the shrubbery and as the contours of the land mutate, so the houses change—because of that alone they will never be identical.

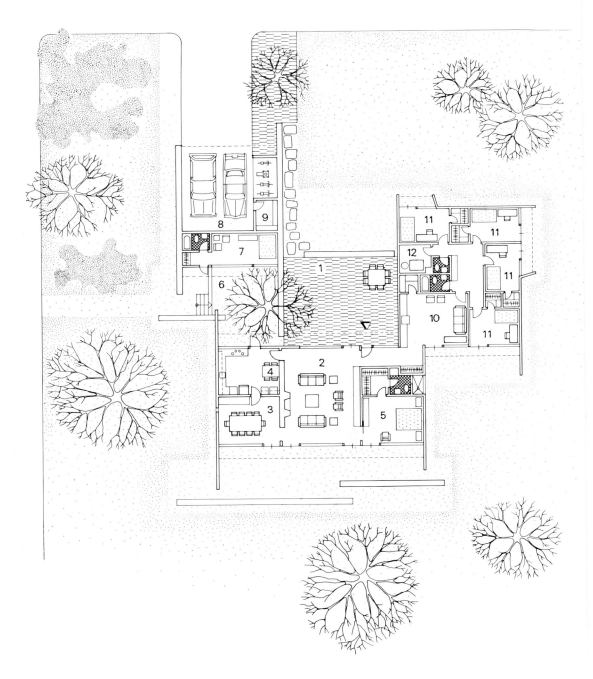

N

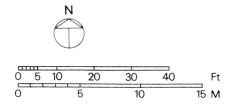

0 5 10   20   30   40   Ft
0   5   10   15 M

1. Courtyard
2. Living
3. Dining
4. Kitchen/Utility
5. Master bedroom
6. Service courtyard
7. Guest bedroom
8. Carport
9. Storage
10. Children's living room
11. Child's bedroom
12. Mechanical

Beckhard House

Glen Cove, Long Island, New York, 1964
Approximately 2,800 square feet
Herbert Beckhard, Architect

At the rear, or south side, a tall fieldstone wall provides privacy for the master bedroom. The children's wing with its living room is set back at right from the rest of the house.
photo: Ben Schnall

Among the most common criticisms of architects who build Modern buildings is that they are seen to be indifferent to context—both the built and the natural ones. When designing his own house for his wife, Eleanor, and four children (Susan, Karen, Tom, and Jane) on a one-acre site of what used to be part of an old estate, Beckhard wanted it to be an integral part of the landscape, so much so that he was determined not to eliminate a single one of the six closely spaced specimen trees that marked the site. Before conceiving a plan, he charted each of the trees—horse chestnut, willow oak, sycamore, two maples, tulip—on the site, essentially weaving the house into the space that remained.

The idea conceptually was to build a house that made itself a part of what was already there. The house and the trees were thought of as inseparable entities. For Beckhard the relationship was clear: he would not like the trees without the house and he would not like the house *as much* without the trees. Beckhard felt that the trees were virtually perfect, "well-worked-out designs." He was even able to get a variance from the town permitting him to place the house six feet closer to the road than allowed by zoning in order to save the 60-foot-high multilimbed horse chestnut tree and integrate it into an interior courtyard, making it an actual part of the architecture; from the roadway the tree appears to spring right out of the center of the building. Aside from a few smaller trees planted for effect and additional privacy, the only special landscaping consists of edges of gravel tracing the perimeter of the house that extend into courtyards and areas of ground cover.

Breuer and Beckhard consistently sought to build houses that intruded as little as possible on the landscape, in terms of both materials and placement. Some of their houses hover a mere six inches off the ground, though Beckhard's is raised to sixteen inches. Indeed, in some cases, such as the Starkey house that is seemingly supported solely by uncannily narrow steel pins, the houses appear almost hesitant to intrude on the earth. Though rendered with a geometric precision certainly unknown in nature, the exterior freestanding stone walls at the front and back of this house (and which are echoed inside) are clearly more in concert with the natural landscape than would be walls of brick or stucco. While searching for the right stone, Beckhard had heard of a farmer in Connecticut who was selling a loose fieldstone wall. Upon visiting it, Beckhard bought the wall, had it dismantled, and delivered to the site. He and his stone mason, Richard Allen, worked as true collaborators on erecting sizable sample walls, one of which was knocked down and the other of which became a permanent wall. Then, on his own, Allen assembled the walls so that the stones' many subtle hues, rugged textures, and distinctive shapes would be highly articulated.

The walls in the front of the house, those that comprise the carport/studio, and the one in the back bracketing the master bedroom are all six-feet six-inches high, tall enough to ensure privacy but never becoming claustropho-

The west side of the house which faces the road is nearly solid. The low fieldstone wall in the foreground absorbs the grade change of the site while also serving to visually extend the boundaries of the living spaces.
photo: Ben Schnall

The entry courtyard is reached by a passageway between two stone walls, perpendicular to each other. The transparency of the house is revealed only when inside the courtyard. (The area has since been paved with bluestone.)
photo: Ben Schnall

bic or overbearing. A low sitting wall runs much of the length of the house in back and appears again at the west side service approach. While it is often used as an informal sitting area, the low wall acts also to absorb the slight pitch of the site so that the interior and exterior appear to be on the same plane. While freestanding fieldstone walls are regular site features of Breuer and Beckhard houses, here they are especially pronounced; from the entrance side they nearly completely shield the house from the street.

Traditionally, main rooms of houses face onto the street. Here the house turns instead into the site—reveling in its topography, fostering privacy, and creating outdoor "rooms" within and outside the envelope of the house. Screening walls that determine private courtyards are commonly used on houses in South American countries. Beckhard's decision to articulate space and maximize privacy in such a way here hearkens to his two-year-long residency in Caracas, Venezuela, in 1959–60 when he was director of a Breuer field office. During that time he was greatly impressed by

the "Spanish" style entry courtyards and their architectural and psychological effect. Here, no material but stone would do. Brick, stucco, or concrete speak blatantly of human fabrication. Stone maintains a primal integrity.

Sunlight plays on the stones throughout the day revealing their richness, but it is at night that the stone walls are perhaps best exploited as they are lit by concealed spotlights—an example of Beckhard's interest in lighting surfaces without revealing the source. Additional light from inside the house spills out through the glass walls providing further illumination to the surfaces.

The stone is brought inside the house as well, and so the dynamic of related interior and exterior spaces is heightened. Though an open plan prevails, a

dramatic stone wall/fireplace again rising six-feet six-inches high and eighteen inches short of the ceiling separates the living room, dining area, and kitchen. A relatively small section of wall adjacent to the monumental fireplace is painted Breuer-blue. Given the rather subdued hues of the bluestone flooring, honey-colored cypress ceilings and walls, white bookshelf wall, and white painted gypsum board, the swatch of blue is startling.

In retrospect, Beckhard would have chosen to eliminate the wall between the kitchen and dining room. In so doing these two rooms and the living room would have become a more singular space. As all architects must do occasionally, the wall was a concession to Beckhard's client, his wife, Ellie. At the time when the

A view from the living room out to the entrance courtyard. Glass walls at both ends expand the space. Multipurpose cabinet at right is typical of Breuer and Beckhard's approach to such units.
photo: Ben Schnall

house was being planned she had been used to the idea of a house needing a defined dining room, living room, and kitchen. Though the kitchen is a distinct room, it does focus on an interior courtyard formed by two walls of the carport/studio structure that opens the room up to the exterior.

One "client" request that Beckhard chose not to heed, however, was to put a door leading from the carport through the stone wall facing the entrance courtyard; to do so would have destroyed the strong visual impact of the wall that results from its length and continuity. Ellie argued for easier access from the carport to the house, especially the kitchen door. Instead, upon parking, one has to traverse the full length of the gravel walkway to the courtyard, a distance that only becomes long in inclement weather. This deliberate delaying of the actual arrival to a house is integral to both Breuer's and Beckhard's belief that an entrance should be as announced as possible. Here a sequence of events has been established. After parking the car in the carport one enters the edge of the street, or the public domain. The gravel walkway represents the transition from public to private areas. Once in the courtyard, one is still outdoors (if not somewhat inside the house) but not part of the public outdoors. Finally the threshold signals an ultimately private domain.

From within, the living room seems to extend well beyond the

A view across the
living room looking
east toward the
master bedroom. All
floors are bluestone
and all windows are
floor-to-ceiling.
photo: Ben Schnall

glass walls, at least to the stone walls beyond. The room in fact embraces the entrance courtyard, in effect another room in itself, complete with its eight-seat table, buffet ledge, and plantings. Toward the rear, or south, the low retaining wall, some twelve feet beyond the glass, becomes an end dimension. A higher, six-foot six-inch high stone wall placed back from the edge of the living room provides privacy for the mostly open master bedroom, separated within the house from the living room by a wide sliding door.

A separate wing to the east, accessible immediately from the entry hall, contains four bedrooms for Beckhard's children and a sunny common room. Each of the bedrooms is modest in size, able to hold only a bed, desk, and chair; built-in dressers in the walk-

Though the formidable stone fireplace separates the living from the dining room, the open plan prevails. A portion of the wall (upper right) is painted the distinctive Breuer-blue. The height of the wall is an echo of the exterior courtyard walls. Ceilings are of honey-colored cypress. Sculptures at left are by Constantino Nivola, an artist whose works figure in several of the houses.
photo: Nick Wheeler

The full effect of floor-to-ceiling glass as seen in the dining room. Granite table is by Beckhard.
photo: Nick Wheeler

On some walls, interior and exterior, wood is placed on the diagonal for bracing purposes and also for visual variety. The overhang maximizes sunlight in the winter and filters it out in the summer.
photo: Ben Schnall

in closets reduce the need for additional furniture. Because the children have access to a bright and airy common room, their bedrooms could be regarded as retreats rather than as complete living spaces. Each bedroom has a floor-to-ceiling sliding glass door which provides direct access to the outdoors. With the exception of the kitchen and studio, all major rooms have floor-to-ceiling sliding windows. The interior hallway that provides access to all four bedrooms receives natural light from a skylight. Beckhard considered installing a door between the children's living room and the hallway leading into the main living room but felt, ultimately, that the zones between children and adult were sufficiently distinct and private.

Courtyards, an open plan, fin walls that embrace space beyond the envelope of the house, a constant reference to the landscape, and thoroughly glazed walls in the living areas make the house seem vast in size, though it is actually modest for a family of six. Beckhard recalls that Breuer, who had no role in the house's design and did not see it until completion, was initially surprised by the size of the house.

There is no question that the house has a strong presence on a site in a suburban area defined otherwise by more conventionally styled houses. Some might think initially that the house turns its back on its neighbors with its fieldstone walls, nearly solid west

facade of white painted board and batten, and landscaping. Instead, the house confirms that what is most important is its site and that its very features should be the objects to be lived with daily. In fact, those same fieldstone walls—as strong as they are visually—actually make the house less conspicuous than any other house in the neighborhood. After all, what could look more natural and endemic to the region than such stone? Both built and natural contexts are acknowledged while the house is allowed to be a wholly original Modern statement. In that sense the Beckhard house shows the ultimate respect to its neighbors.

At dusk the trans-
parent quality and
open plan of the
house becomes fully
realized.
photo: Nick Wheeler

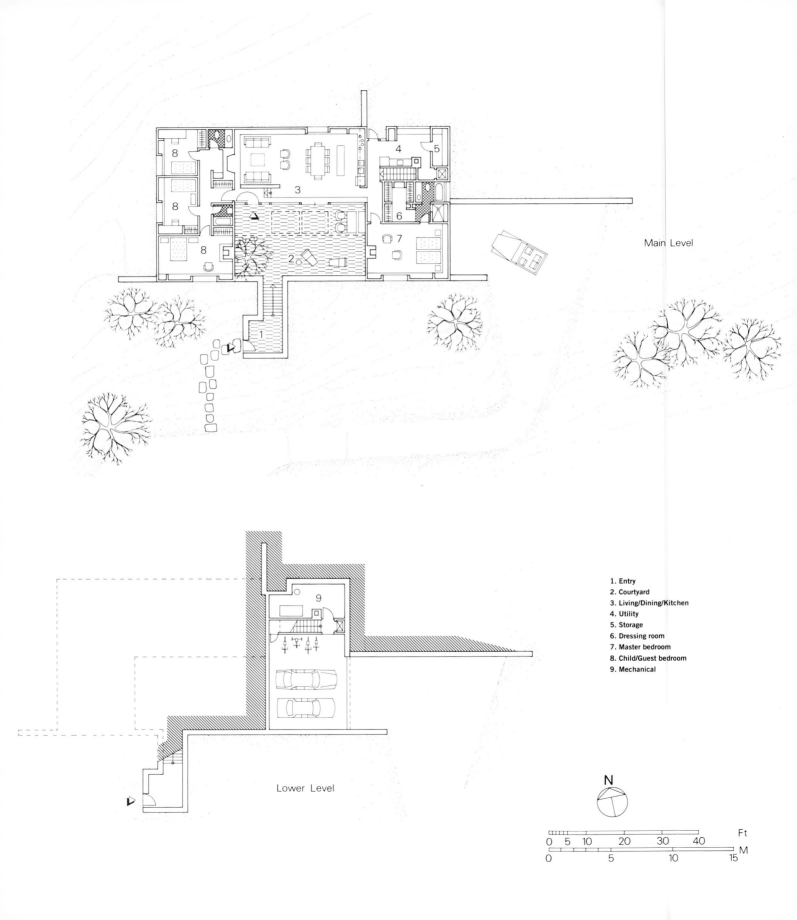

Main Level

Lower Level

1. Entry
2. Courtyard
3. Living/Dining/Kitchen
4. Utility
5. Storage
6. Dressing room
7. Master bedroom
8. Child/Guest bedroom
9. Mechanical

N

0 5 10 20 30 40 Ft

0 5 10 15 M

Stillman II House

Litchfield, Connecticut, 1965
Approximately 2,800 square feet
Marcel Breuer and Herbert Beckhard, Architects

On most Breuer and Beckhard houses the rear facades are the principal ones. Here, the entrance (south) elevation is also the chief view of the house. Two rectangular elements flank—though not symmetrically—the glass wall of the main living area.
photo: Joseph W. Molitor

Given the involved role that many of Breuer's and Beckhard's clients have had in the design of the houses they have commissioned, Beckhard has come to the conclusion that many of them are frustrated architects, with Rufus Stillman being the quintessential example. This was Rufus and Leslie Stillman's second commission for a house in Litchfield with a third to come later. Breuer and Beckhard also designed several factory and administration buildings for Stillman's company, the Torin Corporation. In fact, before assuming control of that company, Stillman had worked for Andy Gagarin, an important client of Breuer and Beckhard's, and it was through Stillman that the architects came to work with Gagarin. Stillman, who was among Breuer's closest personal friends, was as serious about the buildings he had built as he was about adding to his extensive art collection. Beckhard recalls that although Stillman was an enthusiastic, active client, he did not involve himself in a project to the point that basic conceptual matters were compromised.

Like the earlier Laaff house, this house makes an overt though muted reference to a vernacular, traditional style: Mediterranean. As in a Mediterranean house, new or old, the Stillman II house has windows set deeply into the facades. While the first Stillman house was essentially a composition of flat wood planes with windows nearly flush with the wall surfaces, here they are recessed nearly two feet, resulting in a powerful three-dimensional quality. The recessing, together with the dash-and-trowel stucco (a process whereby the stucco is thrown roughly against the surface and worked with a trowel, creating a strongly textured surface), cutouts in the roof, and an entry courtyard that accommodates outdoor living and dining, imbue the house with obvious Mediterranean references, yet there is nothing banal or derivative in the overall design.

Because the house is sited on a hill, the entrance courtyard is reached by a stairway while the rear of the house is at grade level. The driveway curves to the east side where a garage is inserted beneath the house, unusual for the architects. For both Breuer and Beckhard it is important that there be a separation between arriving by automobile and actually entering the house by foot. As a result, the architects avoid putting garages within a house. Breuer reasoned that fumes would leak into the house, which can happen if the garage is not properly sealed, but ultimately it was more a matter of aesthetics and philosophy.

A fieldstone base gives the house a sense of being on a pedestal. Segments of the stucco walls of the house reach down into, and seemingly onto, the rough fieldstone base (some think of it as being just the opposite) which in

The entrance court-
yard is suitable as a
living, dining, and
entertaining space—
and is something to
be seen from indoors.
By being elevated,
the courtyard remains
private from the
ground. Constantino
Nivola bronze sculp-
tures—one of four
castings—accent the
space. The stone
base upon which
the house rests is
visible beneath the
window wall.
photo: Joseph W. Molitor

As is associated
with Mediterranean
architecture, windows
are deeply recessed.
The window is a single
pane of glass that
slides into a pocket.
Stucco and stone
surfaces are woven
together.
photo: Joseph W. Molitor

turn burrows down into the ground.
Though the wall is not pointed or
finished with the degree of
refinement that characterizes most
Breuer/Beckhard fieldstone walls,
it is not completely "dry" either.
The open wall joints were
requested by the client and rather
reluctantly accommodated by the
architects. The resulting wall is
less architectural and more
meadow-like. Though Breuer could
be quite insistent about a design
detail, he did understand the need
for an architect to be resourceful
and to accommodate a client,
especially one so involved in the
architectural process.

Upon passing through a heavy
gate designed by the architects,
one enters a walled reception
chamber from which a brief flight
of stone stairs lead up to the open
courtyard. Within this walled
entryway a person is surrounded by
the textured, robust, multihued
fieldstone; its presence cannot go

unnoticed. The entryway manages
to have a ruinous quality about it
(akin to monuments in Crete or the
Yucatan) while also making the
approach to the house a ceremoni-
ous one.

At the top of this rather
narrow walled entrance walk is the
courtyard. A gravel surface (later
paved with brick), partial overhangs for shading, and outdoor
furniture make the space appropriate as a living, dining, and
entertaining area. Like Beckhard's
own house, a wall of glass allows
the visitor to see into the house
where the wholly open, informal
living plan is revealed. But unlike
Beckhard's house, this one does
not have as strong a sense of being
transparent, for the rear facade of
the house is chiefly solid. In that
sense, the front of this house is
more typical of what are usually
the glazed rear ones of Breuer
and Beckhard houses. Privacy is
maintained by the house's elevation above the site. Windows
look out onto the site but people
below cannot see into them.

A fieldstone wall rises within
the house behind the front door. It
echoes the walls outside, quickly
establishing the outdoor/indoor
living relationship, emphasized in
Breuer and Beckhard houses. But
unlike these outside walls it has a
more finished or crafted appearance. This wall makes it clear that
though there is a link between the
outdoors and the indoors, the interior is ultimately a more refined,
sheltered place. Further establishing this distinction, the exterior

stone base upon which the glass
wall rests is not pointed, while on
its opposite interior side it translates into a finished window seat/
display ledge. A sculptural element
in itself, the ledge traces a significant portion of the main living
area and bedrooms. The stucco
surfacing of the house is also
brought inside and is used for
most interior walls.

The living, dining, and kitch-
en are one open area, and the
entire space has been lowered
slightly, giving the three spaces
additional height. Three bedrooms
to the left of the entry are at a
slightly raised level and their ceilings are a more normal eight feet.
The master bedroom on the opposite side of the house, along
with the utility rooms, remains on
the same level as the living area
(nine feet four inches). Unlike the
Hooper, Beckhard, Cohen, and
other houses, the architects did
not create a central family/
children's room from which there
would be access to the bedrooms.
Instead, an interior hallway links
the rooms. The master bedroom,

Detail of one of
the windows that
slides into a recess.
Artwork within the
recess remains
visible even when
the window is open.
photo: Joseph W. Molitor

Every bedroom has a small fireplace, elevated so that the fire can be seen from the bed. Desk and bookshelves are built in.
photo: Joseph W. Molitor

however, has its own seating area that centers on a small fireplace.

It should be noted that Rufus Stillman, as a result of a World War II injury, has only one leg; yet the house must be reached by stairs and there are level changes within as well. According to Beckhard, Mr. Stillman (who is fitted with a wooden leg) enthusiastically accepted the challenge that these steps would present on a daily basis as a way to dismiss any notion of his being handicapped.

Sealed and waxed red brick flooring is used throughout the house, in part because it contrasts strongly with the off-white stucco walls and dark-stained cabinet wood. The extensive artwork and sculpture that the Stillmans have displayed is made even more conspicuous, as are the area rugs, most of which are based on Alexander Calder designs. The floors remain warm because the brick is laid over a honeycombed concrete slab through which warm air is fed.

The mechanics of the windows are a rather novel Breuer and Beckhard invention—yet another instance of where the architects chose to shun standard products in favor of specially designed alternatives. The single pane windows slide on tracks into a kind of recess in the wall. Within that recess paintings can be hung so they remain visible through the glass when the window is open.

The ceilings are made of painted Homasote, the inexpen-

sive material that the architects used as a wall surface in the Wise house. Partly for reasons of ease in installation, Breuer and Beckhard deliberately emphasized the joints between the rectangular sheets.

The way the house is oriented, how it uses the sun, and that an ever-growing art collection can be easily accommodated shows emphatically that this is a house built to be lived in comfortably. From every elevation the house speaks of precision, geometric purity, simplicity, and harmony— exactly the traits one could attribute to typical Mediterranean houses. But because this is a thoroughly Modern house it has complete freedom to hearken to such a traditional style and form and yet be its own composition. Unlike virtually all other Breuer and Beckhard houses where opposing solid and glazed panes meet, here there are no such planes. Corners are solid and every elevation is a blend of wall and window. Breuer and Beckhard clearly have no qualms about departing from their own customs. Though themes occur repeatedly, their architecture is, ultimately, one without rules.

The principal living
space as seen from
the kitchen. Stone
is brought inside as
partial flooring, a
screening wall, and
a continuous window
seat. Interior wall
surfaces are stucco,
and flooring through-
out is red brick.
photo: Joseph W. Molitor

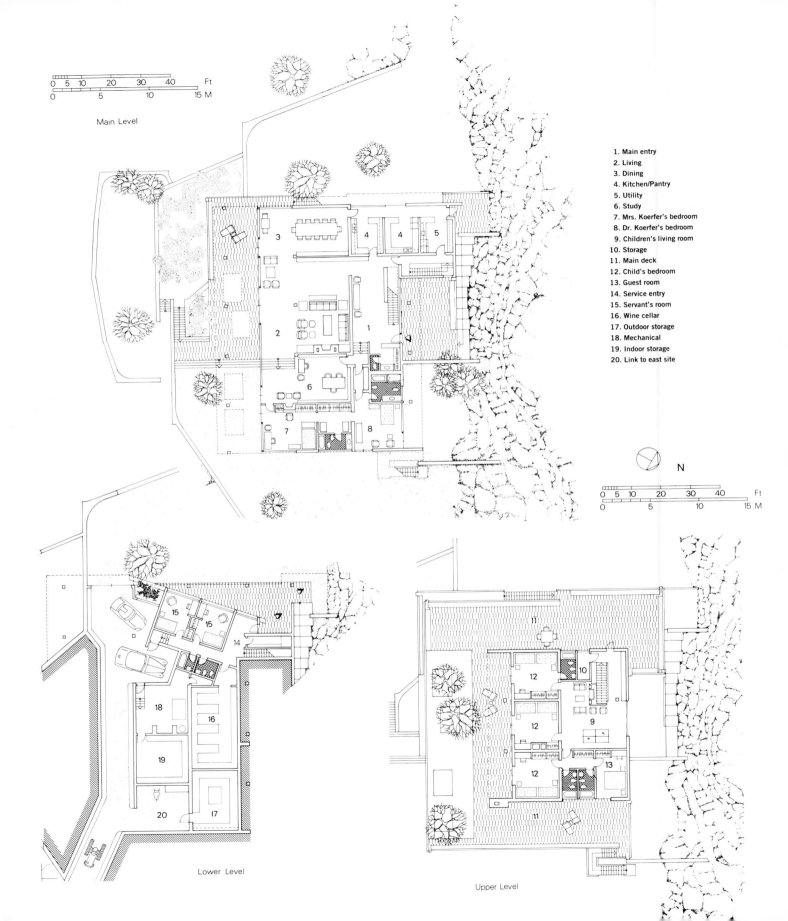

Main Level

0 5 10 20 30 40 Ft
0 5 10 15 M

1. Main entry
2. Living
3. Dining
4. Kitchen/Pantry
5. Utility
6. Study
7. Mrs. Koerfer's bedroom
8. Dr. Koerfer's bedroom
9. Children's living room
10. Storage
11. Main deck
12. Child's bedroom
13. Guest room
14. Service entry
15. Servant's room
16. Wine cellar
17. Outdoor storage
18. Mechanical
19. Indoor storage
20. Link to east site

N

0 5 10 20 30 40 Ft
0 5 10 15 M

Lower Level

Upper Level

Koerfer House

Lago Maggiore, Switzerland, 1966
Approximately 14,000 square feet
Marcel Breuer and Herbert Beckhard, Architects

On the east side, there is room for a lawn. The walnut-trimmed windows add a degree of color to the facades, comprised otherwise of bush-hammered concrete, granite, and glass. Local quarried granite is configured much like typical Breuer and Beckhard fieldstone walls. A dramatic flight of stairs leads from the terrace to the grade. Window at far left is Mrs. Koerfer's bedroom.

When Jacques Koerfer, the former chairman of BMW, and his wife, Christina, approached Breuer with a commission, they had been living in an old Gothic house near Bern for nearly thirty years. It was there that Dr. Koerfer began to collect twentieth-century paintings. "About 1960 I thought about building a modern house as a frame for my growing collection," Koerfer has said. Though he had considered Alvar Aalto for the house, it was a photograph of a Breuer interior that Koerfer came upon in a book that convinced him who he wanted for the project. "In this book I found one room . . . the living room in the Robinson house . . . whose atmosphere, I

sensed, showed that Marcel Breuer could probably do a house for me," Dr. Koerfer recalls. A visit to the extraordinary site in Ascona, which overlooked the Lago Maggiore toward Italy, and a subsequent visit by the Koerfers to Breuer's New York office solidified a personal and working friendship. Not long after completion the house was given the American Institute of Architects National Honor Award, a highly coveted distinction rarely given to an individual house.

Both Breuer and Beckhard were initially surprised by the assignment in that the site already contained a large house in excellent condition; but Dr. Koerfer was intent on tearing it down and

building a new structure, one that would not have to rely on the existing grading or foundations. Among the strongest stipulations were that the house accommodate the couple's three 10-year-old sons (triplets), maintain privacy between the children and the adults, and show off to the best advantage Dr. Koerfer's enviable collection of modern paintings: Legers, Rothkos, Picassos, Mondrians, and others. In some ways, the design requirements included features associated with an art museum. Breuer's Whitney Museum was nearing completion at the time, so both architects were well attuned to the requisites of a museum building and how best to reveal artwork.

While the razing of the existing residence freed Breuer and Beckhard to impose their own vision, the hilly, arrestingly steep site was a fixed challenge. Surely, the hillside terrain and the vista over Lago Maggiore were to be celebrated but it was necessary for Breuer and Beckhard to fashion usable, level outdoor spaces for the occupants.

The house's structural system consists of an exposed concrete frame with all exposed interior and exterior surfaces reflecting a careful crafting of the material. The concrete was poured with special care into molds comprised of smooth one-inch by four-inch wood boards tightly jointed. When the forms were removed the concrete was bush-hammered by hand to reveal the multicolored stone

A detail of a portion of the south facade. A series of broad steps connect various levels of garden. Openings in the upper level allow for trees to grow through; the exaggerated overhang creates a protected space beneath.

aggregates. The same exterior structural system and the bush-hammered surfaces find their way inside as well—as walls, baseboards, door trims, moldings, a fireplace, freestanding columns in the living room, and elsewhere. At this point, the architects were well acquainted with exposed architectural concrete technology. To date the architects had erected large-scale, wholly concrete structures, including the UNESCO headquar-

ters in Paris and St. Francis de Sales Church in Muskegon, Michigan (the University of Massachusetts Campus Center would be a later example), but the Koerfer house represented a smaller-scale application of the material and technology. (Breuer had worked with architectural concrete on numerous other earlier projects.)

With no local fieldstone available, the architects used local quarried granite in combination

with concrete for exterior walls. Breuer and Beckhard seldom used quarried stone because they did not like the square edges that resulted from being hewn out of quarry beds with machines. The rectangular pieces were placed randomly so as to look as much like fieldstone as possible. Like the bush-hammered concrete, the granite, too, is carried inside where it is used for a massive fireplace in the living room.

From the spacious roof deck there is a view out over Lago Maggiore toward Italy. The cantilevered steps on the exterior staircase appear to float in midair.

The transparency
of the full-height
window wall and
the way it fosters
the relationship be-
tween exterior and
interior is apparent
in one of the seat-
ing areas of the
living room.
photo: Yukio Futagawa

Though extremely subtle, the
walnut wood used for all window
frames imbues the exterior with a
degree of color not found in many
Breuer and Beckhard houses.
Against the muted granite stones
and concrete, the reddish brown
wood is especially sharp.

Most ceilings within are
concrete, and their smooth side-
board form is apparent. Because
each board used for the mold has
its own character—graining, knots,
and so on—and its own rate of
water absorption, the surface that
results is a varied one.

Like many Breuer and
Beckhard houses, here again it is
the rear elevation that becomes
the principal one—the facade that

is most highly articulated or
opened up to the elements. Yet,
because of the sharp incline on
which the house is sited, that
facade only becomes fully visible
from far out on the lake. A sketch
prepared during the design stage
(see page 101) reveals that view,
ultimately an idealized one because it is so difficult to see in its
entirety.

The Breuer and Beckhard
solution of entering a house from
the front but quickly winding up at
the back is especially pronounced
here. Yet, at this house, because of
the unique topography, visitors
actually arrive at what is the side
of the house, walk under a porch to
the front, and then upon entering

quickly move to the rear. Since one
approaches the three-story house
up a steep grade by means of a
winding road, the lower level is
given over to the functions of
arrival and parking. Mechanical
facilities, storage areas, and
servants' quarters are also situated
there. A stepped ramp leads from
the driveway to an entrance
courtyard. At this point visitors are
still not aware of the true drama of
the site; when working with a site
that affords beautiful views, Breuer
and Beckhard have a penchant for
postponing the revelations of these
views as long as possible. Upon
entering the spacious entrance
area one is confronted with a large
white plaster wall; it not only manages to hide the view beyond but
functions, with the aid of museum-
type lighting, as an important
display area—on both sides—for
paintings.

Ultimately, the lake and
mountains beyond become startling fixtures in the living area,
which is marked by two seating
areas. The adjacent dining area
also has two seating areas, one for
larger gatherings and a smaller
intimate one in a corner often used
for breakfast. Here as well as in
Mrs. Koerfer's bedroom, window
walls form a glass corner, a design
element that appears infrequently
in Breuer and Beckhard houses. A
pantry, kitchen, and laundry room
are arrayed behind the dining area.
A minimal flight of wide steps
from the living area leads to Dr.
Koerfer's office where from his
desk he is able to look out toward

The main seat-
ing area of the living
room is dominated
by the granite fire-
place. Museum
lighting reveals, as
shown here, paint-
ings by Leger and
Mondrian. Granite
floors are relieved
by soft, carpeted
areas. Chairs in the
foreground are by
Charles Eames, a
furniture designer
favored by Breuer
and Beckhard.

the view. A hallway/room containing office equipment leads to Dr. Koerfer's bedroom while another door leads to his wife's bedroom. A dressing room with a bathroom off it provides another link between the two bedrooms. Two exterior stone walls of varying length that butt into the rugged, natural terrain stretch out from Dr. Koerfer's bedroom creating a closed garden. The missing third wall is the natural rocks of the site.

The third level is essentially devoted to the three children, all of whom have equal-size rooms looking out over the lake. A guest room is situated in the northeast corner. While two exterior staircases lead to the main level, a grassy area and a large terrace, the interior staircase, an eerily floating series of cantilevered granite pieces with no risers and roughly hewn edges, leads from the entry to a playroom that acts as the children's living room. As in the Beckhard house and other examples, the playroom gives the children a strong sense of having their own place in the house, and yet it also functions as a family room. The generous roof surface with a substantial overhang relieved by strategically positioned cutouts makes for generous outdoor paved living spaces that hearken to the earlier Staehelin house and the even earlier

An interior detail showing the built-in cabinets, wall paneling, precast bush-hammered door frames, and continuous stone floor.

In the background is the study fireplace, defined by a precise geometry. Beyond is the door to Mrs. Koerfer's bedroom.

A sketch of the house made during the design process as it would appear from out on the lake. Due to the steep terrain, it is not possible to photograph this elevation, which is actually the principal one.
Illustration: Alexi Vergun

The interior staircase, connecting the main and upper levels, is composed of rough-cut granite steps.

Robinson house. An independent structure located approximately 50 meters up the hill reached by a flight of stepping stones contains the pool pavilion with additional entertainment facilities. The interior there receives most of its light via four large skylights.

As Beckhard sited his own house around the existing trees on his site, so he and Breuer did much the same here. Extant trees grow up through cutouts in the overhang created by the roof terrace. Plantings beneath are nourished by rainwater and sunlight that come through the openings; from the upper deck the tops of the trees become unusual landscape features. By bringing the trees into the very footprint of the house the relationship between the interior and the exterior of the house is an intimate one.

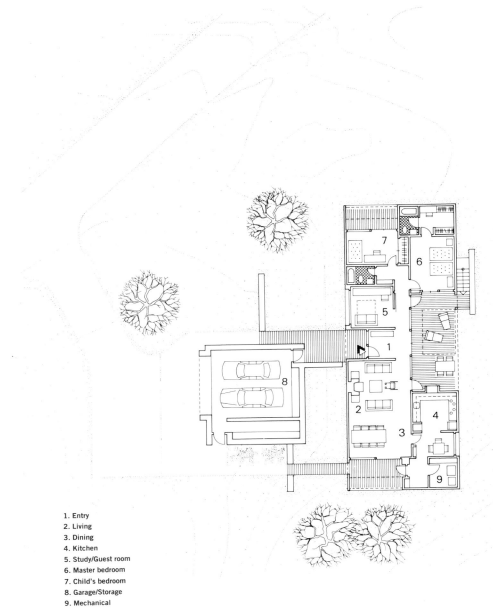

1. Entry
2. Living
3. Dining
4. Kitchen
5. Study/Guest room
6. Master bedroom
7. Child's bedroom
8. Garage/Storage
9. Mechanical

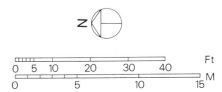

N

0 5 10   20   30   40   Ft
0   5   10   15 M

Reed House

Danbury, Connecticut, 1968
Approximately 2,200 square feet
Herbert Beckhard, Architect

The house cantilevers over the rugged topography. Porches on the west and south are contained within the envelope of the structure.
photo: Fred Picker

Among the key ideas in this house was for the client to be able to follow the sun. George Reed could be on the east deck of his bedroom in the morning, the main deck in midday, and the west deck off the dining area in the evening. This desire to court daylight and the outdoors was due in large part to Mr. Reed's confinement to a wheelchair. Having ready, self-gained access to the outdoors was a major concern. Indeed, the plan with its wide central circulation area, limited doors, and materials such as smooth quarry tile for the floor acknowledge the special needs of one in a wheelchair. As Lillyan Reed recalls, "We had been living in a traditional style house and it was so cumbersome going from room to room that we had enough experience to know what those needs were going to be. There were certain rooms in the old house that George couldn't even get into; we knew about interior spaces and the ability to get outside"

Yet, the house was not so tailored to Mr. Reed's needs that it could not work successfully for his wife and young son. Beckhard recalls that George Reed, more than just about any other client, understood the spaces, their relation to each other, as well as every detail and dimension on the drawings. Ironically, very soon after moving into the house Mr. Reed died, due to complications related to his polio. Both he and his wife had established a strong friendship as well as professional association with Beckhard, and so Mr. Reed's death was an especially sad and resonant event. Lillyan continues to live in the house. She remembers visiting the house constantly at various stages in its construction. "George was so involved that were he able to come out with hammer and nails he would have been out here building it himself. Although it was George's house as a project he also knew that it was everyone's house to live in." To all but perhaps Lillyan Reed, it is unnoticeable that the house was designed to accommodate a handicapped person.

It was a virtually universal design axiom at the time—dictated in America by federal guidelines—that homes for handicapped persons be placed on slabs at grade level, permitting easy access in and out. Beckhard decided early on, however, that Mr. Reed "deserved to get off the ground," that a man forced to be on the ground all of the time should instead have the ability to rise above it and have a different experience. Part of that experience would mean being self-reliant. Also, because wheelchairs do not move on lawns, Beckhard felt that a house up in the air with wood decks and porches reached by minimally sloped ramps would facilitate outdoor living. As a result, given its floating nature, the house has been informally likened to a tree house (a remark also

From the west, one
of the two bridge/ramp
connectors is visible
leading to the service
porch. While the
house hovers over the
irregular terrain, the
stone garage is de-
cidedly earthbound.
photo: Ben Schnall

made by the Robecks when de-
scribing their house).

The house is situated on a
rocky and irregular site with sur-
rounding patches of woods—a further consideration for raising the
structure. The house is cantilevered at both the east and west
ends and rests on a recessed base
in which there is storage space and
the heater room. The garage with
its heavy fieldstone walls is earthbound, while the house just beyond is reached by gentle ramps as
it hovers over the terrain. The north
facade is marked only by a narrow
horizontal window in an otherwise
blank wall of stained cedar boarding. It is on the other three facades
that the house opens up and detail

becomes important. The sudden
transition from ground to air, the
use of ramps, and a restrained entrance facade versus a highly articulated rear are features reminiscent of the Starkey house.

Most of the exterior surfaces
of the house consist of cedar wood
boards, which contrast subtly with
the fieldstone walls of the garage,
those at the back of the house, and
the fieldstone base upon which the
house rests. An existing fieldstone
wall assembled without mortar and
laid generations ago to mark a
pasture boundary runs essentially
parallel to the south facade. Its
free-flowing, tumbledown
character is all the more conspicuous given the rigorous geometry of

the house. In fact, that wall was
one of the reasons the house was
located the way it was, and it is
clear that Beckhard wished to take
full advantage of it. Whether it be
trees, hillsides, or relics like this
old wall that speak of past
occupation, Beckhard strives to
preserve original features of the
landscape.

As for access, the idea was
that Mr. Reed could drive his car
into the garage and enter the
house unaided through a door that
opened onto the main entrance
ramp. A second ramp on the west
side of the house, placed in front
of the house but concealed largely
by the garage, leads through a
deck into the kitchen; it serves

both as a service entrance and as an alternative informal entrance to the house.

The main deck, situated at the center rear of the house, is the house's focal point, and as a result is an announced space. Much of the interior of the house is visible from it and it is clearly an extension of those areas. None of the decks is a wholly open form. Free beams extend from the roof line to complete the form of the house, not unlike similar elements at the Schwartz and Breuer/Bratti houses. As a result, the decks come to resemble courtyards more than notches in the envelope of the structure. A pass-through window allows food to be passed directly from the kitchen to the main deck to accommodate outdoor dining. Sliding glass doors provide access to the main living area, entrance, and master bedroom; there is indirect access to a small study/ guest bedroom. A short flight of stairs off the main deck leads down to a grassy area. All three decks—the son's, another off the dining area, and the main one— extend living spaces and create highly individual places. Duffy Reed, for instance, had his own private deck on the east side, an important extension of his otherwise compact room.

At its conception, the layout of the house was essentially the reverse of what it is now. Though it made sense for the kitchen instead of the bedrooms to be on the road side of the house, Mrs. Reed saw the need for easier access from the

The east elevation. Old existing stone walls that marked the boundaries of the site were retained. The main entrance ramp connects the house to the grade.
photo: Ben Schnall

At the rear the house becomes a strong horizontal line across the rolling landscape. A stone wall at right conceals a stairway to the grade, while an old stone wall essentially runs parallel to the house.
photo: Fred Picker

A view of the living
room from the din-
ing area. Cedar
boarding used on the
exterior is brought
to the interior, but
used on the hori-
zontal. The bush-
hammered fireplace,
containing wood and
record storage nooks,
is accented by a
beam of natural light
that comes through
a skylight.
photo: Fred Picker

garage to the kitchen and so the
house was flipped. Unlike in most
Breuer and Beckhard houses
where garages are purposely well
separated from the house, here
that is not the case—a clear concession to the real needs of the
client. As in many of the architects' houses, such as Geller II
and Stillman II, the objective was
for the living, dining, and kitchen
areas to be one space. "In those
days, as a young woman who I
suppose was obsessed that some-
body might see some dirty dishes
on the counter, I couldn't quite
deal with that concept. I needed a
closed kitchen, and even wanted
at one point a traditional separated
dining room." Beckhard convinced
Mrs. Reed that, for the living room
and dining room, it was preferable
to have one large, airy space rather
than two compartment-like rooms.

Among the most dramatic details in the combined living/dining
area is a skylight just in front of a
cast-in-place bush-hammered
concrete fireplace, smaller than
most of the architects' fireplaces
because of the modest size of the
room. A concentrated beam of
natural light illuminates the highly
sculptural fireplace and spotlights
the chief conversational area of the
living space. The skylight, in consort with the two other sources of
natural light (south and west), provide the room with a changing
quality of light throughout the day.
Much of the light-colored cedar
wood on the outside is brought
inside, while other interior walls
are white painted gypsum board.

Floor tiles are a soft gray. Ceilings
are composed of acoustic tiles with
a rough texture that obscures
joints and resembles plastered
stucco. Given the muted colors of
the materials, the Breuer-blue that
appears on a wall of the study/
guest room and in the master bedroom is noticeably vibrant.

In summing up her twenty-
five years in the house, the resi-
dent says that "we always have the
feeling that we have access to the

outdoors, no matter what the sea-
son. There's a feeling of always
living outdoors while still indoors
and safe and protected."

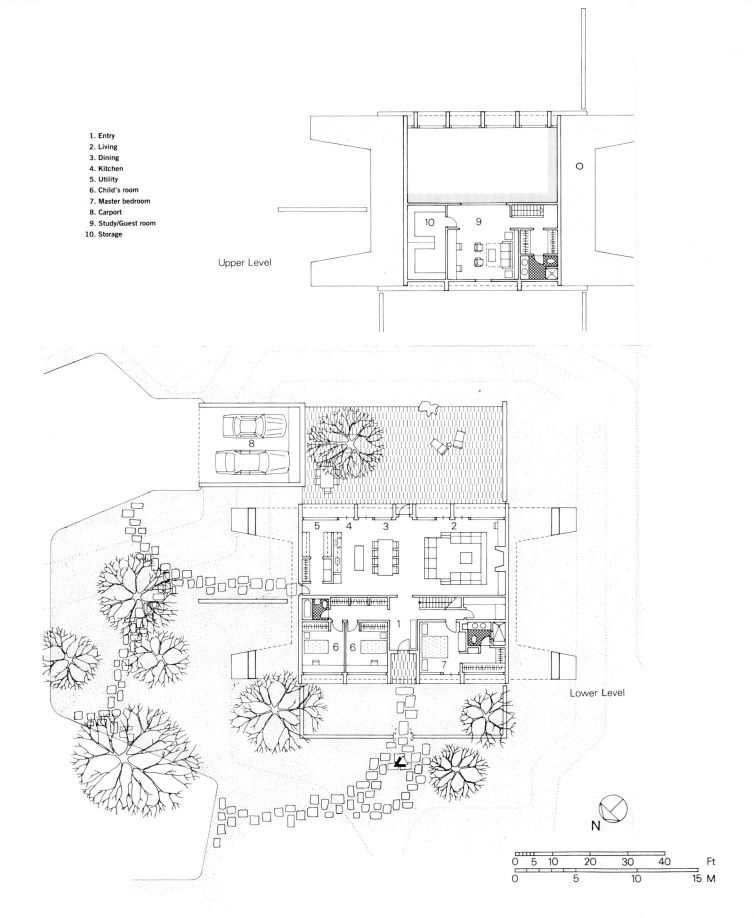

1. Entry
2. Living
3. Dining
4. Kitchen
5. Utility
6. Child's room
7. Master bedroom
8. Carport
9. Study/Guest room
10. Storage

Upper Level

Lower Level

N

| 0 | 5 | 10 | 20 | 30 | 40 | Ft |

| 0 | 5 | 10 | 15 M |

Geller II House

Lawrence, Long Island, New York, 1969
Approximately 4,500 square feet
Marcel Breuer and Herbert Beckhard, Architects

The entrance or north facade is more private than the rear one. Bedrooms face onto an enclosed courtyard. The window at the top provides a secondary view from the guest room/study at the upper level. The placement of the house is due, in part, to the existing specimen trees.
photo: Ben Schnall

When Bert and Phyllis Geller commissioned Breuer to do a house for them in Lawrence, Long Island, in 1945 neither they nor Breuer could have imagined the impact the house would have on the town—indeed on the whole of American residential architecture. The house and separate guest wing structure that came to occupy the site on Ocean Avenue, with its opposing "butterfly" roof forms, low-slung sweeping envelope, unpainted cypress wood walls, "floating" car-port, and elevations marked by trapezoidal and horizontal bands of windows (see page 16) was for some residents a shocking intrusion and to others a refreshing revolutionary design. As

with most wealthy American suburbs, Lawrence had for decades been distinguished by its stock of staunchly traditional houses—Colonials and Tudors especially. The Gellers, who were only in their early thirties when they decided to commission Breuer, were clearly adventuresome people. Modern houses simply did not exist in suburbia in 1945. For the twenty-year-old Beckhard back from Navy service in the Pacific and with less than two years of engineering school before that, the sight of that house in his hometown in 1946 was an epiphany. He credits the Geller house with his decision to act on his latent interest to become an architect.

Some twenty years later after their children had grown up, the Gellers, still taken by Modernist aesthetics, wanted to build a new and different house in the same area. A dramatic six-acre site just down the road was distinguished by a wooded area, which made a transition to a picturesque marshland sanctuary, and eventually beyond that to the ocean.

Breuer and Beckhard had designed a house ten years earlier that was to be built in Aspen, Colorado. The conceptual plan and most of the working drawings had been completed when the client died unexpectedly. Breuer, pragmatic as a businessman who was head of a firm with employees and as an architect aware that he had designed a good house, asked the Gellers if they would be interested in the design. They were and after a number of design adjustments, to suit both their needs and the new site, the house was begun. Also, given the architects' relatively new interest in concrete technology, technical matters had to be resolved that in turn dictated design changes.

The house takes as its form a parabola. As a result, the space within is generous, uninterrupted, and bright with sunlight. The main facade, at the rear of the house, takes in the spectacular marshland view. In effect, this entire elevation is a two-story-high screen that is structurally independent of the poured concrete shell that comprises the house. The various geometric forms act not only as a

The main or rear facade faces south. Rough board-and-batten-formed concrete walls screen the terrace from neighbors. Windows of the board-and-batten-formed sun screen are so deeply recessed that each element becomes distinctive. The rectangular elements are in direct contrast to the sweep of the arch. The object at right is a sculpture by Constantino Nivola.
photo: Tom Breuer

The symbolic entry to the courtyard and house is reminiscent of Japanese forms. The photo is taken with the door open, revealing the view one is presented with upon entering.

practical screening device but as a frame for the scenery beyond. The importance of how the shape of a window determines how a view is presented is often unappreciated. Here that dynamic is exploited. Views are captured through distinctly horizontal, vertical, and triangular openings. Although the configuration of shapes formed by concrete sections appears structural in form, the design is ultimately the result of aesthetic concerns. For instance, Beckhard's ingrained dislike for pure squares makes for some shapes that appear at first to be square but in fact are not. There is a horizontal emphasis and Breuer and Beckhard did much to make the shapes as pronounced as possible without the composition becoming chaotic. The architects were also intent on offsetting elements, giving them as much definition as possible; to do so each pane of glass is deeply recessed. No vert-

ical members reach from top to bottom and there is no sense of routine division in the overall facade.

The entrance facade, which faces north, is more secretive and restrained. Board-and-batten-formed concrete walls five-feet six-inches high encase a rock garden/courtyard onto which bedrooms look. Seemingly hovering in space, a concrete archway—evocative of traditional Japanese forms—links the walls and formalizes the entrance to the house. Since this archway centers on the front door, when it is open one can look directly through the house. A nearly square solitary window is punched in the center of the parabolic arch. Where there is predominantly glass on the south facade, here most of the surface is of painted stucco, subdivided by concrete members.

The walls of the entry court, and those at the rear on the east and west sides that allow for privacy for the outdoor terrace from adjacent neighbors, provide a horizontal foil to the sweeping form of the house. The wall on the east side forms a side of the carport, which is sunken slightly so that all walls are on the same plane.

Breuer and Beckhard, who are recognized for reveling in the engineering aspects of a house sometimes as much as the aesthetics, indulged here in the technical, to the point where the technical becomes the aesthetic. The rough concrete walls are made deliberately conspicuous, and the very shape of the house is meant to be startling. The gaps the arch makes as it hits the ground beckon like caves. The thrust or outward push of the arch is absorbed by

The straight-on
south elevation fully
describes the para-
bolic arch that forms
the house. A paved
area allows for in-
formal outdoor living.
photo: Ben Schnall

The living and
dining areas and
kitchen are con-
tained in a single
uninterrupted
space. The conver-
sation area is sun-
ken. Flooring is
bluestone set in
an irregular pat-
tern—a treatment
and material
requested by the
Gellers as it had
been used in their
first house. The
inner surface of
the arch is covered
with a rough cork
surface for acousti-
cal reasons.
photo: Thomas Breuer

these points of support, which are tied together by underground tension members. Partitions that connect to the arch include slip joints allowing for vertical movement of the arch as it rises and falls with temperature changes. The concrete side walls of the house and sun screen are separated from the arch by gaps containing compressible neoprene sponge.

The concrete of the arch and sun screen is formed using tongue-and-groove interlocking boarding, which leaves its imprint on the concrete. Just as conspicuous are the ties that hold the wood forms together. The holes they make in the finished concrete have not been fully filled in, giving the house a kind of raw, almost unfinished look. Yet, despite that imprecision and crudeness, the pieces of bluestone that comprise the terrace are rigorously geometric. The bluestone flooring inside the house is randomly composed, however, of irregular pieces.

Informality is the key to the interior plan. The main area's living and dining area and kitchen function as a single space. The conversation area is defined not only by furniture placement but by its being sunken; in so doing, there is an even greater sense of height to the room. One side of the pit functions as a sitting and display ledge. The sunken area is carpeted, in part for acoustical reasons as the echoes within a domed vault can be strong. Behind a kitchen wall of cabinets is a storage area and laundry facility.

Three bedrooms are situated on the entrance side of the house behind the gypsum board wall that splits the parabola. The ceilings in those rooms are flat because within a second-floor area is a large

View toward the kitchen from the dining area. Kitchen elements are a charcoal gray, while the architect-designed table is a salt and pepper granite, at which are placed Breuer "Cesca" chairs. The spun-plastic lamps are vaguely Japanese in feeling.
photo: Ben Schnall

studio/study. This room's ceiling is defined by the arch. The space looks down onto the main living area and is announced by an opening with angled sides.

The ceiling in the main area is made of cork painted white; in the bedrooms the material is left in its original dark-brown state. Not only is it a material much favored by the architects, but it also has acoustical benefits as it reduces echoing. The cork is actually the liner of the form in which the concrete shell was molded. During construction it had support pins coming out of it; when removed, the cork remained fastened to the concrete.

There is a strong interplay between the house as a free-flowing sculptural entity and as a practical, albeit radical, solution for a structure that is meant to take advantage as fully as possible of the drama of its site. In many ways the rounded, soft form of the house echoes the site, one that evolves from woods to marshland to ocean. Unlike the original Geller house, this one is set back considerably from the busy road and concealed by heavy growth. Were it as conspicuous as the first house, it, too, might have caused a kind of tempered suburban furor given its rather eccentric form.

A view from the
guest room/study
at the upper level.
Only a balcony
separates it from
the main space.
The varied window
forms frame dif-
ferent views.
photo: Ben Schnall

1. Entry
2. Dining
3. Living
4. Kitchen
5. Master bedroom
6. Guest bedroom
7. Deck
8. Garage
9. Courtyard/Future studio

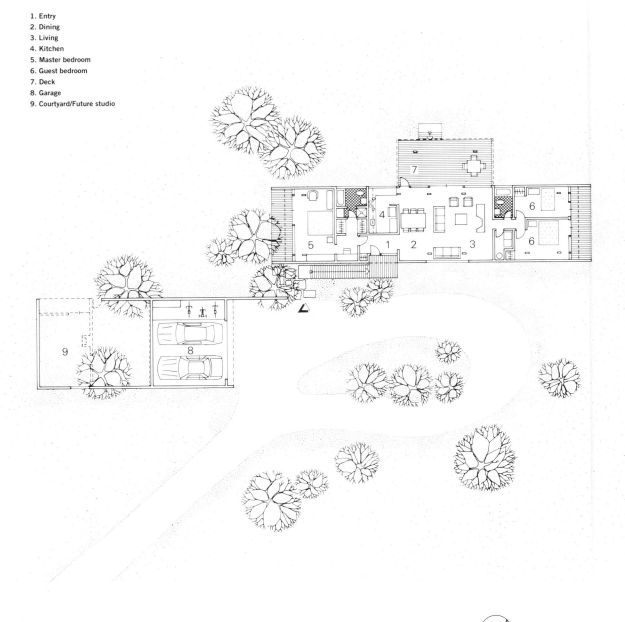

N

Ft
0 5 10   20   30   40
M
0   5   10   15

Rosenberg House

East Hampton, New York, 1969
Approximately 2,700 square feet
Herbert Beckhard, Architect/Jeff Vandenberg, Associate

Upon approach the house all but disappears in the landscape. Long horizontal wood surfaces are interrupted only by the entry with its ramp, a band of windows, and garage doors.
photo: Joseph W. Molitor

One could almost miss this house in the landscape, it is so much a part of it. Beckhard's objective was to let the house settle in with the landscape, to be as little an intrusion on it as possible. Unlike so many of the opulent weekend houses that have been built in the Hamptons, the Rosenberg house is a simple retreat in the woods, scaled for the weekend needs of Arnold and Rochelle Rosenberg. For Arnold Rosenberg, living in a small house faced with wood that would noticeably shrink in winter and swell in summer "was exciting, almost like being on a ship."

Amid the typical eastern Long Island secondary growth of dense smallish trees, the house appears as an uninterrupted hovering horizontal statement. Given the pronounced vertical elements on the four-acre site—the lines of the trees—Beckhard felt that one long horizontal line would be an appropriate counterpoint. In so

doing, the line effect of the trees would be maximized. Consequently, while the cypress wood house becomes an intimate feature of the landscape, it manages also to contradict it. For the client, an eminent commercial photographer, the house is "something easily maintained and indigenous to its environment."

The house consists of two separate rectangles that appear to merge from certain points of view as the result of an exterior wall that overlaps the edge of the house with that of the garage; what looks to be a freestanding wall is one wall of the garage. The garage is designed with a rear courtyard around which a future guest house/studio could be built. The entrance side of the house is marked only by an asymmetrically placed entrance, reached by a ramp, and a narrow, horizontal band of windows highly placed to ensure privacy from the road and protec-

tion from the east sun. Aside from these windows, the facade is reminiscent of the Hooper house in that all that exists is a squarish oversize entry cut into an otherwise blank, solid facade of a horizontal form.

Other than the alternating portions of vertically and diagonally placed wood planks on the facing of the house, the other immediately apparent exterior detail is the house's hovering quality. It "floats" two feet above the ground by means of a raised concrete foundation and cantilevered floor construction, in part because the site is often damp but also as a way of further minimizing its presence on the landscape. The structural system of the house employs exposed laminated columns and beams. Their use allows for substantive cantilevers at the north and south ends of the house. The ramp approach to the entrance imbues the structure with a nautical sense, appropriate given the water setting just beyond.

While Breuer and Beckhard always configured their houses to take advantage of important vistas, they also reserve views for certain rooms. This desire for withholding views for maximum impact is apparent in many houses—Geller II, Staehelin, Koerfer, and here. To the west is an expanse of wetlands vegetation and a tranquil pond, onto which the combination living/dining area looks. The three bedrooms, two of which are located on one side of the house to ensure privacy from the master bedroom,

On the west, the
main deck remains
largely covered
by an overhang,
while an adjacent
lower deck (not
shown on the plan
as it was a later
addition) receives
considerable sun-
light. Narrow, slit-
like windows mark
the kitchen and
bathroom facilities.
photo: Joseph W. Molitor

have views oriented away from the pond to the woods. The idea was to save the view of the pond for occasions when one is in the living/dining area. If people are seated on the main deck off the living/dining area, guests in the bedrooms can still have privacy on their decks. Like Beckhard's Reed and Cohen houses, every bedroom and central living space has access to a deck. Here the central deck is covered but is augmented by an adjacent wholly open one that receives considerable sunlight. Exterior living is so encouraged that the kitchen is only a semi-enclosed galley space, efficient for cooking but not for lingering in. A door immediately off the kitchen leads to the rear deck where many meals are eaten.

Because the house rests on a concrete base and slab, bluestone flagging could be used for the floors of the centrally positioned living/dining area. A fieldstone fireplace set asymmetrically in the area (the opening and terra-cotta flue are in turn positioned off-center) acts as a shield to the part of the house that contains two guest bedrooms. People have to circulate around the fireplace to enter the other rooms. This highly sculptural element is constantly confronted in the course of daily living. This aspect is central to Breuer and Beckhard houses: key design features—be it the envelope of the house itself, a fireplace, a sun screen—are deliberately positioned to ensure examination.

The dark stained laminated columns and beams placed upon the raised foundation that allow for the cantilevering are strong interior elements, as strong as the vintage furnishings—Mies van der Rohe chairs, a Scarpa couch, a rare Breuer Isokon reclining chair, a Beckhard dining table. Like the McMullen house, dark stained wood structural members are juxtaposed with lighter natural wood and white gypsum board walls. The Rosenbergs like the rugged quality of the posts and beams and the way they come to articulate space. "Their placement in the rooms forced us to put furniture around them and created little seating areas which were very nice."

One of the most important endorsements, albeit a subtle one, of the house came from a close neighbor, the late Gordon Bunshaft, the renowned architect at Skidmore, Owings and Merrill. Aware that his house and

The deck off the master bedroom remains private from the other more public decks, which are seen at left. Placement of elements is often dictated by trees.
photo: Joseph W. Molitor

Bunshaft's were the only two Modern ones in the area, Rosenberg suggested to Beckhard that they pay an impromptu visit to the infamously gruff architect to see his house. As Rosenberg recalls, "I introduced Herb, and Bunshaft, with his ever-present pipe in his mouth, asked grumpily if we were having problems with the construction of something in my house. He asked what those 'funny posts' were that were coming out of the foundation. But during the construction of my house, I'd sometimes find his car in the driveway as he was looking to see what we were doing. Years later after I had sold the house, I ran into him in a supermarket and he said simply, 'That is a nice house.' For Bunshaft that was being ebullient."

Rosenberg also recalls the builder of the house, Frank Johnson, who began work on it when he was seventy-nine. Johnson had worked on many of the grand houses of East Hampton, including the imposing Maidstone Club, built like an English manor house. "He had never worked on a Modern house before and thought that it would be one of the great things to do in his life before he died. My wife and I were lucky in that we had two people we admired greatly [Beckhard and Johnson] who understood what it was we wanted, in the deepest personal sense, for the house."

View from main deck looking south. Sun and shade are equally accommodated.
photo: Joseph W. Molitor

The intimate living space focuses on a rugged and simple fireplace, which acts as a shield for the guest area beyond. In the right corner is a rare Breuer Isokon chair. Other furnishings include Breuer "Wassily" chairs and sofas by Mies van der Rohe. White painted walls contrast with the expressed posts and beams, all stained dark.

photo: Joseph W. Molitor

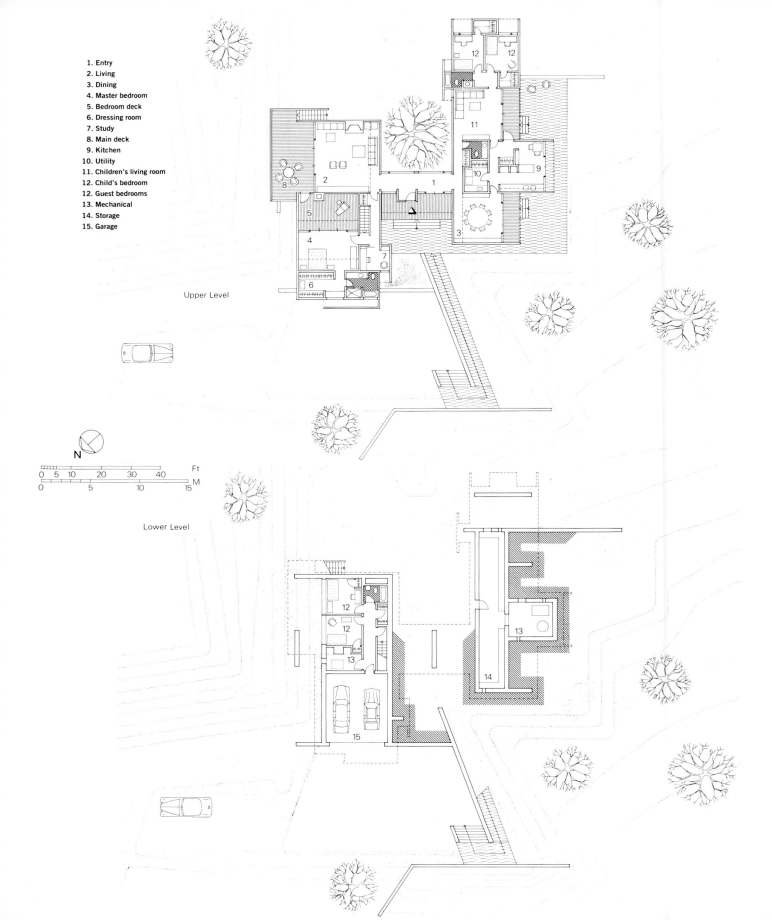

1. Entry
2. Living
3. Dining
4. Master bedroom
5. Bedroom deck
6. Dressing room
7. Study
8. Main deck
9. Kitchen
10. Utility
11. Children's living room
12. Child's bedroom
12. Guest bedrooms
13. Mechanical
14. Storage
15. Garage

Upper Level

N

Ft
0 5 10   20   30   40

M
0   5   10   15

Lower Level

South Orange, New Jersey, 1971
Approximately 4,100 square feet
Herbert Beckhard, Architect/Donald Cromley, Associate

The house is actually entered from the side. A stairway from the sunken driveway leads to an angled walkway to the entrance. The house is marked by a play of forms, some oriented north-south and others east-west; the elements are connected by a simple, narrow rectangular element: the entrance.
photo: Gil Amiaga

The site on which this house is now situated had lain empty for so long that it was assumed that the lot was unbuildable. Few architects or clients could imagine a house fitting comfortably into a place marked by a steep ravine, uneven and dramatic grade changes, a smattering of trees, a northern exposure, and neighboring houses close by on three sides. The Cohen residence is a prime example of the fact that conventional, traditional houses are difficult to build on hilly, rugged sites, whereas Modern houses—by nature of their not having to follow any rules—can be accommodated on such challenging sites more readily and freely. As a result, this

distinctive, rambling house imposes itself on the site with a forcefulness atypical of other Beckhard and Breuer houses. Rather than deferring to the landscape, here the house seeks to dismiss it.

Houses like Beckhard's own residence and Breuer's second New Canaan home seek to be as unobtrusive on and as accommodating to the landscape as possible. Here, the house exploits every feature in the landscape and, ultimately, conquers it—a lower level fills in a deep cavity in the lot, the center of the house is configured around a large existing tree, decks and whole portions of the structure are built out over

steep falling grades, a massive concrete retaining wall that braces the earth has an important visual impact.

From the quiet suburban road, the house appears virtually windowless but, as with many Breuer and Beckhard houses, glass is reserved for every facade but the front one where privacy is an issue. Upon entering the driveway, the visitor is struck by the painted scored concrete block wall and another wall of poured concrete. While Beckhard admits that he could have "and maybe should have" faced the purely concrete wall with cinder blocks, its chief purpose is one of support, to hold back the earth. The seemingly disparate, differently shaped elements of the house are faced with painted pine siding. A long walkway of bluestone, angled to the entrance facade of the house and reached by a series of steps from the driveway, leads to a simple entrance terrace; the paved area wraps around all parts of the house that meet the ground. Actually, given its position on the site, the house is entered at the side. A black front door is set within a box-like entry area comprised of Breuer-blue painted surfaces, which in turn is set into glass walls.

Unlike most Breuer and Beckhard houses, the entrance foyer is formal in scale and function. It is a place apart from the living areas and it is from here that all points in the house are reached. Upon entering, one is keenly aware

The back or private side. The paving of the entrance walkway traces those elements of the house that meet the grade. The dining room at left features its own deck.
photo: Gil Amiaga

An angled walkway makes for a dramatic approach.
photo: Gil Amiaga

of being raised above the ground; only the entry, kitchen, dining room, and living room are at grade. That fact, coupled with glass walls on both sides of the foyer, and the use of elevated decks, provides an uncanny sense of floating. An immediate issue is whether one is more a part of the inside of the house or the outside.

While the bi-nuclear separation of master bedroom from those of the children has been established in earlier Breuer and Beckhard houses, living spaces here are also separated. One wing of the house contains the living room and the master bedroom suite with its office/study, bathroom, and large dressing area. A stairway amid this complex of rooms leads to the lower level which contains a garage, mechanical and storage rooms, and space for two additional bedrooms if needed. To the other side of the entrance foyer is the dining room, kitchen, children's living room, and two children's bedrooms. The children's wing is further segregated from the adult zone of the house by a door that leads from the kitchen to the outside; children can enter and have direct access

to their living area and bedrooms, a greater asset as children get older. Though rooms still flow into each other, they are more rigorously delineated than in other houses. This was emphasized here, in part because the clients like to entertain and the delineation of rooms allows for greater circulation among large gatherings of people.

Because the site, except at the rear, has few expansive, private, or level areas, decks become a major component of outdoor living activity. The main deck off the living room connects with a gate to an interior courtyard/deck off the master bedroom. The borrowed light that comes through as a result is crucial in illuminating what would otherwise be a dark room. Other shallower decks, which are completely covered as they are recessed in the building, are situated off the dining room and off the children's living room; both lead to on-grade outdoor areas which are an extension of the entrance paving. These decks become effective transition points from the interior to the exterior paved terrace. Beckhard deeply recessed all glass surfaces for privacy, sun control, and to add to the house's sculptural quality.

The house is essentially flat-roofed except for three dramatic sloping surfaces, the first use in a Beckhard house. Not only do these surfaces make the master bedroom, living room, and dining room taller (in the living room, for instance, the ceiling rises from a low point of eight feet to eleven

feet), but they bring natural light via clerestory windows. Though it faces north, the living room, for instance, receives an ample supply of southern light from its clerestory. Cohen comments that he especially loves the house at certain times of the day, such as after work at cocktail hour, because "there is light coming from everywhere."

After twenty-one years in the house where they raised their two children, Arthur and Francine Cohen have recently completed a restoration of the house, totally faithful to the original. Breuer-blue surfaces on the outside and inside of the entrance area and on various doors throughout the house are especially vibrant. A notoriously difficult shade to duplicate, the color was mixed using an original paint chip from one of the doors. Furnishings have remained in their original form or have been redone identically. Wood floors throughout, however, have been restained a slightly darker shade to further offset the white walls and wood ceilings. Durable, reddish brown

The dining room is situated in its own wing and acts as a clearly defined room. The soaring angled ceiling and the diagonally positioned wood panels give the room strong dynamics.
photo: Gil Amiaga

The ceiling of the living room rises from a low point of eight feet to eleven feet. Though the room faces north, it receives considerable southern light through clerestory windows. With most of the architects' fireplaces, flues are exposed, but here it becomes an integral part of the stucco wall. The main deck acts as an effective extension of the living room space.
photo: Gil Amiaga

Welsh quarry tiles on the bathroom, kitchen, and entrance foyer floors complement the wood floors yet serve as subtle transitions to rooms where such water-resistant surfacing is needed.

The Cohens point out that "we have always been Modern oriented. I wanted a squarish stone house just like Herb's," says Mr. Cohen, who with his wife, Francine, have been longtime friends of the Beckhards, "and I was very surprised when I saw the model and plans for this house." Because of the site little stone could be used since it needs considerable ground support. Instead, much of the house utilizes lightweight wood framing cantilevered to seemingly float over the ground. An even sense of space and mass is established, clearly a logical response to the conditions of the terrain. With its three projecting roofs, cantilevered sections, and seemingly independent wings, the house appears like a small village of individual, abstract dwellings. Within, though, the house readily accommodates the life a single family, maintaining that fine balance between privacy and togetherness.

1. Entry
2. Kitchen
3. Dining
4. Living/Sleeping
5. Study

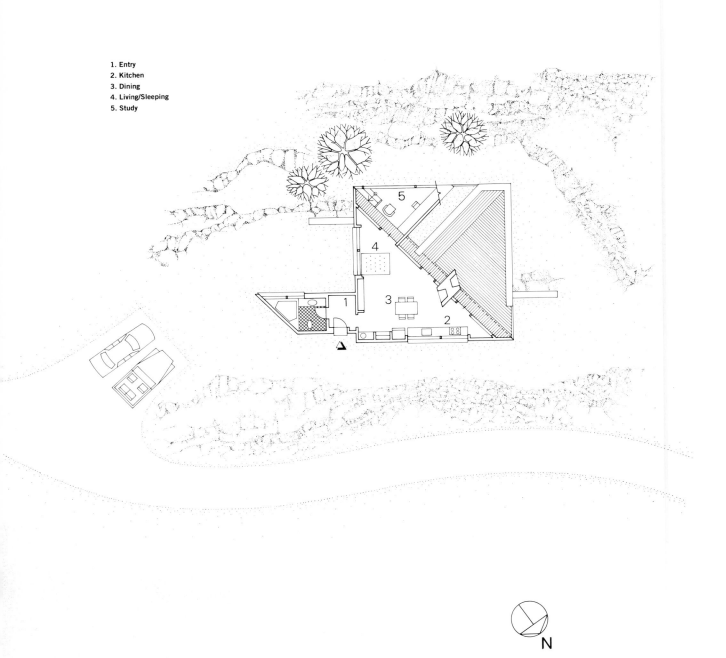

Ft
0 5 10   20   30   40

M
0   5   10   15

N

Gagarin II House ("Big Sur")

Big Sur, California, 1975
Approximately 600 square feet
Herbert Beckhard, Architect/Thomas Hayes, Associate

The deck, on the west, almost equal in size to the interior living space, is defined by the two-sided bush-hammered fireplace and the bench that traces the triangle.
photo: Joshua Freiwald

As seen from the south, the house virtually disappears into the landscape. The single pitch of the roof follows the slope of the terrain.
photo: Joshua Freiwald

Despite having a large and rather famous house in Litchfield, Connecticut, that Breuer and Beckhard designed in 1955, the client, Andy Gagarin, was eager for a rigorously spare and small West Coast retreat. His wishes for a natural, Spartan existence went to extremes: at first he did not want a washing machine in the house, wishing instead to walk down to the Pacific Ocean to wash his clothes; also, he wanted an outhouse instead of inside facilities. Recognizing that this was a once-in-a-career chance, Beckhard designed a stone outhouse, but regrettably it was never built because of a California law stipulating that such facilities must be built inside a house.

Situated on a spectacular coastline with the ocean on one side and the Sierra Madres Moun-

tains on the other, Beckhard was emphatic that the house exploit the landscape and temperate weather conditions and that the form of it essentially adhere to the steep terrain. The soaring angled roof does that as it follows the incline of the hillside, while the raised deck at the rear allows the topography to flow right under the house. As at the Wise house, the terrain is allowed to virtually become a part of the house. While the triangular shape is a decidedly foreign one on the landscape, it presents a minimal interruption on the hillside—so much so that from the southwest side, the house is virtually lost as it becomes immersed in the hill and foliage upon it.

Both the interior and the exterior living spaces are identical in that they are, in a sense, dimensionless. Just as the deck embraces the limitless vista of ocean and mountains, the interior with its minimal division of spaces becomes one wholly open space. The small size of the house almost obliged Beckhard to take his in-

terest in open plans to extremes.

Beckhard fitted the essentially one-room house with a deck almost equal in size to the interior living space. The triangular deck is edged with a continuous bench that stops just short of the complete triangle—as good an example as any of Breuer and Beckhard's predilection for creating subtle imbalances in a composition (entrances that are not centered in a facade, fireplaces that are situated off to the sides, windows that are never pure squares). Sliding floor-to-ceiling glass doors make inside/outside movement effortless.

Another especially conspicuous effort to make outdoor living similar to indoor is the massive, though well proportioned, bush-hammered concrete fireplace. Less overtly sculptural than most of the architects' fireplaces, its dual opening serves both the deck and the central living portion of the interior. In the evenings the outdoor fireplace becomes an important gathering spot as it provides heat. From the inside the

A section of the
multipurpose room
is used for sleeping.
Glass expanses
contrast with narrow
slit windows, which
maintain privacy
from the approach.
photo: Joshua Freiwald

flue is hidden in what appears to
be a roughly hewn cube resting on
the fireplace top. Its texturing,
somewhat rounded edges, and
deliberately imprecise geometry
conjure up adobe-like forms.

Within, the house has full
views of the ocean, mountain, and
yard—vistas up and down the hillside. Two narrow bands of horizontal windows follow both the
kitchen wall and the one behind
the bed. Even though the steep
incline of the hillside is just beyond, the windows provide a pan-
orama of the indigenous topography and foliage—so close in fact
that the views are like those seen
in dioramas in natural history
museums.

The soaring ceiling does
much to make the house feel
larger than it really is. Beckhard
also felt that by using only one
material for all surfaces, cedar,
that the house would not seem
small because there would be no
competing materials. Only the
carpeting could perhaps be considered another material;
Beckhard would have preferred
stone floors but the client was
concerned about stone being too
cold since there was no heating
system in the house other than
the fireplace.

With one of the triangle's
corners higher than the other two,
the resulting sloped roof creates a
distinctive interior space in which
all of the elements—cooking,
sleeping, living, eating—are informally distributed. Though small,
each area of the house has its own

character as a result of the varying ceiling heights. The window in the bathroom comes down to the edge of the tub allowing its user to look out at the Pacific Ocean. Another large triangular window fitted in the southeast corner of the house at the maximum height point of the pitch captures views of the mountains. This window and another triangular one also on the southeast wall appear at first merely eccentric in shape. However, their shapes are determined by the line of the roof, angle of the cedar boarding, and edge of the house. Extravagantly geometric as they are, they are much like the windows in the Bornhorst house where window form is also dictated by roof form.

Though largely dictated to by the lay of the land, Beckhard was able to fully exploit here his interest in exaggerating and extending the approach to a house. Upon leaving the highway that runs above the house, visitors pull into a small parking area from which they must descend on a steep path to the entrance. The entrance is positioned adjacent to the highest point of the triangle so that the full drama of the house is revealed immediately.

Beckhard admits that he wanted the house to be dynamic and dramatic, but not so much that it became restless. Because of the simplicity of materials used, the house has great tranquillity. While its unnatural shape could have made the house seem an intruder on the hillside, its place-

ment and the way it responds to its surroundings guarantees instead that the structure fully honors it.

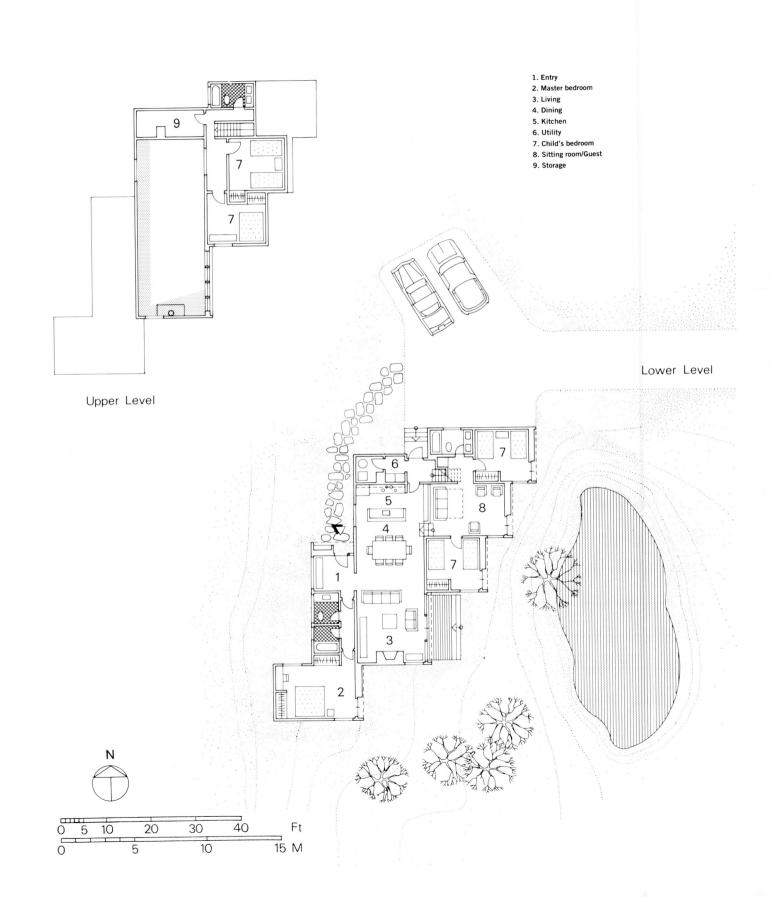

1. Entry
2. Master bedroom
3. Living
4. Dining
5. Kitchen
6. Utility
7. Child's bedroom
8. Sitting room/Guest
9. Storage

Lower Level

Upper Level

N

| | | | | | | |
0 5 10   20   30   40   Ft
0   5   10   15 M

Bornhorst House ("Twelve Bikes")

Queeche, Vermont, 1979
Approximately 3,200 square feet
Herbert Beckhard, Architect/Dirk Bornhorst, Associate

A side view from the south reveals the illusion of many different roofs, though the house is actually fitted with one simple shed roof form.
photo: Nick Wheeler

It is not often that an architect would be willing to collaborate with another on the design of his own house. When the Venezuelan architect Dirk Bornhorst decided to build a winter retreat for his family in Vermont he was aware of what he wanted the house to be—in form and plan—but was also willing to admit a certain lack of knowledge about building in a climate vastly different from the tropics where he was used to practicing.

Upon visiting the site in 1977, Bornhorst began sketching a rudimentary conception of the house. His early plan grouped the five major rooms of the house so that each took in prominent views

to the east and south. Also, he envisioned a series of complex, intersecting roof planes on a house of many parts. The shape that resulted embodied a design principle he encouraged in his classes at the Central University in Caracas: "rhythm with abstract values" and a "play of light and shadow." Recognizing that he wanted an "American architect who could transform these ideas into working plans" he turned the project over to Beckhard, whom he had met and befriended in 1960 while Beckhard was living in Caracas for two years working on a major urban complex that, ultimately, never reached the point of construction.

Once the design concept for

this house was resolved between the two, Bornhorst assumed the role of Beckhard's client, not exactly a common situation among architects. Bornhorst's overall form and preoccupation with dramatic pitched roofs appealed to Beckhard. But Beckhard also knew that much had to be changed to make the house work in harsh Vermont winters, as well as to accommodate the special requirements of wood frame construction (a system Bornhorst had not experienced). Aside from relatively minor changes like repositioning bathroom fixtures away from outside walls and creating larger overhangs of the roof to get icicles farther away from the edge of the house, Beckhard recognized that the very shape of the roof required the most important change. With the heavy snowfalls and build-up of ice typical of the region, it is detrimental to have intersecting roofs that require flashing. Leaks and rotting will occur.

Beckhard's solution called for a simple continuous pitched roof form. As if done with a cookie cutter, the roof is simply cut to fit the plan of the house. When a conventional pitched roof is cut this way, distinctive forms result. Because the plan of the house is comprised of several parts positioned at different planes, the multiple roof forms that Bornhorst had envisioned remained, but had been transformed into a workable solution.

As in many Breuer and

Trapezoidal windows follow the form of the roof. While windows on the south are nearly flush with the facade, on the east they are deeply recessed. There is an interplay of vertical and diagonally placed cedar boarding.
photo: Nick Wheeler

Beckhard's schematic drawing for the roof, a single continuous form irregularly cut by a number of vertical planes.

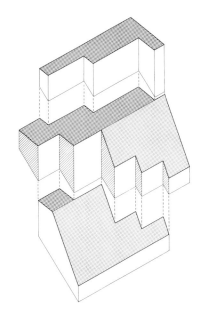

Beckhard houses, views, no matter how splendid, are often saved for certain rooms for maximum impact. Bornhorst had originally thought of having two large identically sized windows in every main room that looked south into dense woods and east onto a man-made pond on the property, a key element in the overall site design. The house that Beckhard designed orients the major windows to the pond, but smaller, quirkier, more intimate windows effectively frame the forest views. Some of those latter windows are trapezoidal; their shapes are dictated by the line of the roof. The major windows are of door height, most of which can be slid open horizontally allowing direct access to the oudoors from every room. The west side of the house is built close to a steeply rising hillside, visible particularly from inside through a window in the kitchen area and another in the large vestibule. The house's combination of fixed and operating windows is revealed especially in the kitchen where two small horizontal projected windows operated by handles are placed below a fixed window.

In looking at the east elevation, the house has a pronounced rhythm and drama. Its five elements, containing master bedroom, living/dining area, family room, and two bedrooms are juxtaposed to one another. While the roof has an upward sweep over three of the projecting building elements, it is reversed over the other two where the roof slopes downward. As a result, the full height of the roof is revealed while also giving the house a conspicuous counterpoint. Without this roof differentiation, the five parts of the house, marching along the site as they do, could make for a daunting, even perhaps too repetitive building. The element containing the living/dining area has a clerestory window that also relieves the facade by opening it up at its tallest point. The five individual elements, especially the one with the clerestory window, are similar to those that comprise Beckhard's Cohen house; but here they are part of a single building envelope rather than the seemingly independent functioning units at the Cohen house. (Another important distinction is that in the latter the units are positioned in different directions.) Also, each of the window groupings in the five parts here are deeply recessed. This not only helps shelter the house from cold winds and glaring sunlight but also imbues the facade with a sculptural sense.

An important feature of the principal facade is the use of fieldstone panels adjacent to each of the sliding glass doors. Though it would have been more economical to have used the same gray-stained cedar boarding of the house, Beckhard fought hard to convince the client that the fieldstone walls would bring a needed textural contrast to the facade. To emphasize both structural bracing qualities and the forward thrust of each of the house's sections, the cedar

The east facade looks onto a man-made pond. As the roof reverses its pitch over two of the five parts, a strong counterpoint results. Stone panels are placed adjacent to full-height windows on an otherwise all-cedar house.
photo: Nick Wheeler

The double-height living/dining area. The fireplace is of the same local fieldstone as on the outside panels.
photo: Nick Wheeler

siding is placed diagonally on the north and south sides and vertically on the east and west. Forced by budget considerations Beckhard used standard inexpensive asphalt roof shingles, though he would have preferred "good old Vermont" slate tiles.

The house is meant to be used by two families, who, conceivably, would alternate visits. (Because there were two adults and four children in each family, with one bicycle per person, the house came to be known as "Twelve Bikes.") An open loft space, reached by a steep staircase, contains two bedrooms and a full bathroom that could be used by the children should other guests be visiting.

The living, dining, and kitchen areas are contained in one informal continuous space. A stone fireplace of the same stone as on the exterior panels with an exposed terra-cotta flue is at the far end of

the living room. In keeping with the Breuer and Beckhard inclination to separate living from sleeping zones, the master bedroom is situated at the extreme southwest corner of the house. At the main entry to the house Beckhard fashioned a particularly large vestibule to accommodate skis and winter gear and provide a place for the storage of firewood.

While Beckhard positioned the family room as a central pivotal space within the sleeping zone, as is common with many of the architects' houses, here there is also direct access to the dining and kitchen areas, making the room a true family space and not one exclusively for the children.

In keeping with the budget, and recognizing that the house would be subleased throughout the seasons by unknown renters, the

interiors are more routine than in other Breuer and Beckhard houses. Floors are carpeted instead of being of bluestone or brick, and all walls and ceilings are painted gypsum board. Yet the interiors are never dull, for the varying heights of the ceilings throughout make each room and area different.

Given the principal role of Beckhard, the collaboration of Bornhorst, and the input of Oscar Schnell who with his family would be sharing the house with the Bornhorsts, "Twelve Bikes" reflects and embodies several separate concerns. Yet, as Bornhorst remarks, "out of this pool of ideas emerged a dynamic and interesting solution, which at the same time was so amazingly simple."

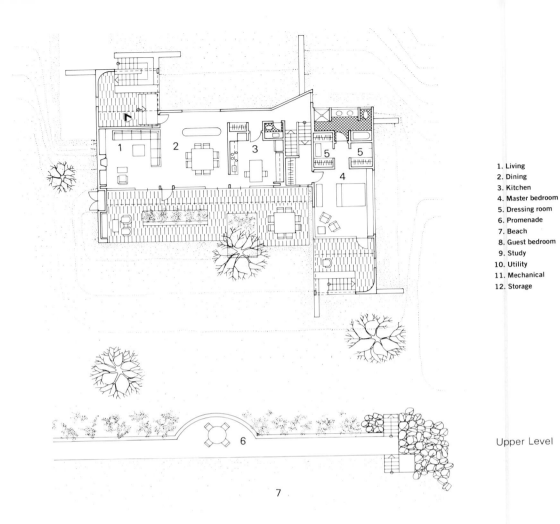

1. Living
2. Dining
3. Kitchen
4. Master bedroom
5. Dressing room
6. Promenade
7. Beach
8. Guest bedroom
9. Study
10. Utility
11. Mechanical
12. Storage

Upper Level

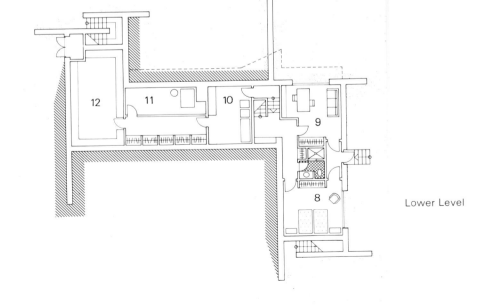

Lower Level

N

					Ft
0	5	10	20	30	40

M

0	5	10	15

Schwartz House ("Green Farms")

Westport, Connecticut, 1984
Approximately 3,400 square feet
Herbert Beckhard, Architect/Robert Kupiec, Associate

The rear facade or principal view, the south elevation faces onto Long Island Sound. A pure glass corner (upper right) is formed in the master bedroom.
photo: ⓒ Andrew Appell 1984

Though it is a near-blasphemous term in Modern architecture, this house follows a split-level plan. It made sense for Beckhard to configure the house this way, for by raising a significant section of it up in the air, he was able to ensure privacy from neighboring houses on the narrow site and to maximize views of Long Island Sound, to which the house has direct access. Privacy between guest quarters and the master bedroom suite was easily accomplished with level changes. In addition, it made sense to take advantage of the gentle slopes that characterized the three-acre site and allow the house to follow the terrain rather than try to conquer it.

This house, so named for a nearby academy and the road on which it is situated, is built on an old existing foundation. Fire had destroyed a previous large manor house and all that remained on the site was burned lumber and a foundation embedded in the ground. While that extant foundation determined the general configuration of the house, Beckhard did not feel constrained by it. An old servants' quarters building with a three-car garage remains some distance away at the front of the site. In devising the overall site plan of the house, Beckhard planted a thick grove of trees to hide that building, a rather unattractive structure that differs wholly in style and spirit from the house. Parking remains quite remote from the house, a clear example of Beckhard and Breuer's tendency to have both owners and visitors walk to a house rather than drive right up to it.

As a result of the hilly terrain, similar to that on which the Stillman II house is sited, the front of the house rests on a base of rough stone, while the rear is at grade. Also, like the Stillman house, the main entrance is reached through a stone-enclosed stairway in which one confronts the vigorously textured stone. The rest of the house is finished in an off-white rough textured stucco, some of which carries to the interior.

An unusual and prominent feature of the house is its two porches, one that acts as an entrance plaza, and the other as an outdoor seating area and extension of the master bedroom. Both are exuberant—in shape, scale, and impact—and both are marked by window-like openings. The open-air porches serve to capture and frame outdoor space; the notion is both philosophical and literal. Beckhard has been a longtime admirer (and friend) of the late architect Louis Kahn, and he cites Kahn's notions of creating "borrowed spaces" with "borrowed light" as a personal goal in his more recent buildings. Whether or not that was a conscious decision here, the porches do accomplish all that. Space and light get trapped in a limited area; that area

A view from the
elevated master
bedroom porch.
photo: © Andrew Appell
1984

remains open and free and yet also gets used as a true living space.

Within, the house is a typical Beckhard open living/dining plan except that the kitchen is held private from this main room by a partial wall behind which is the stove and oven. A brief flight of stairs leads up to one-half of the split level containing the large master bedroom suite with its porch and large dressing and bath areas. The dramatic view of Long Island Sound onto which the bed-room faces is enhanced by a pure glass corner—a rare phenomenon in any Beckhard or Breuer house. From the main level, the staircase leads down to the other half of the split level containing a guest bed-room, which has direct access to a terrace and the beach, a study, and utility rooms. Given the water-front site it is not surprising that views are captured as fully as possible and that outdoor living spaces are integral to the plan; for the clients, who are New York apartment dwellers and who have never lived in a house before, such features are especially welcome.

Immediately discernible from the exterior side entrance, and from the interior as the visitor looks down the length of the house from the entry porch, is an angled corner. While Beckhard could have kept the plane of the front of the house strictly linear, he created this notch to open up the stairway and provide for a more spacious landing area, as well as to create an element of surprise. Though situated elsewhere and accom-plishing very different effects, this angle is reminiscent of the skewed entrance Breuer devised for the first Gagarin house.

While Beckhard's interest in a largely private front facade and glazed rear one prevails, the notion seems to become less important in his later houses. Here the front is chiefly solid, though there is a sizable glazed opening and the familiar horizontal bands of windows appear at the top of the second story and cut into the stone of the lower level. The main living areas—kitchen, living, dining, and master bedroom—are as open as possible, with full walls of windows and direct access to the south-oriented terrace. An exterior stair-case off the bedroom porch, in fact, leads directly to the grade.

All built-in furnishings were designed by Beckhard, a typical

on a fieldstone base, the all-white stucco house has a special prominence on the site, and its full expanse and form are instantly revealed. At the rear, the site slopes down to the water's edge; when viewed from the beach, the house's porch becomes even more imposing, especially against the low horizontality of the house's adjoining element.

The glass corner in the master bedroom minimizes the separation between exterior and interior spaces.
photo: © Andrew Appell
1984

procedure for Breuer and Beckhard houses. Particularly noteworthy are a granite-topped buffet table in the dining area, an ingenious tiled table in the kitchen, and storage units that are part of the headboard in the master bedroom. The clients, who do not have children, often eat in the kitchen at the tiled table which also functions as a work surface and wine storage facility. Bluestone flooring to which Beckhard admits he is "addicted" (tiles this time) is used in the living, dining, and kitchen areas, as well as on the outside terrace and porches.

The focus of the living and dining space is a stucco wall with a fireplace and niches of varying size carved into it. This same stucco wall extends to the exterior where another niche, one used for seating, appears. This extension of the wall serves also to shelter the main terrace and to screen the patio/terrace from adjacent neighbors. From it and from the extreme width of the wall there, one can see that Beckhard clearly was interested in avoiding a "thin" edge in favor of massiveness and substance.

Both of the porches seem stage-like, raised on pedestals or plinths of sorts, supported by columns, and defined by beveled corners. These qualities conjure up images of ancient built forms. By being elevated (at the front facade)

The strong in-
door/outdoor
relationship fos-
tered by floor-to-
ceiling glass is
emphasized in the
compact but ef-
ficient kitchen.
Gray speckled
ceramic tiles are
combined with
gray enamel
cabinets and
bluestone flooring.
Center object is
a combined
breakfast table
and wine storage
facility.
photo: © Andrew Appell
1984

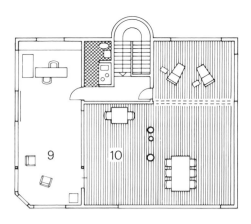

Roof Level

9

10

1. Entry
2. Living
3. Dining
4. Kitchen
5. Utility
6. Boat storage
7. Guest bedrooms
8. Master bedroom
9. Studio/Study
10. Deck

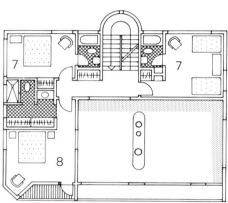

Middle Level

7 7

8

N

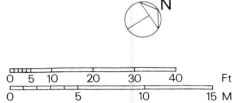

0 5 10   20   30   40   Ft
0   5   10   15 M

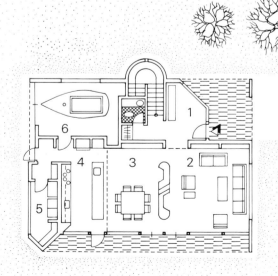

Main Level

6

1

4 3 2

5

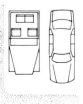

Vasiliou House ("Osprey Nest")

Fishers Island, New York, 1984
Approximately 3,900 square feet
Herbert Beckhard, Architect/Hasram Zainoeddin, Associate/Michael Wu, Associate (construction phase)

The principal elevation is the east facade. The three-story box is punctuated with openings both glazed and unglazed. At the upper level the sky appears through a sizable opening. At the intermediate level a small porch is inserted at the master bedroom. A long narrow opening provides a secondary view from the main living space.
photo: © Andrew Appell 1984

The prevalent play of openings and solids is strongly revealed at the entrance side, where the form is pierced only by an opening to the sky and a recessed entrance. The expressed curve of the stair landing is the only projecting element on any of the house's four sides.
photo: © Andrew Appell 1984

The notion of imbuing a house with sculptural elements is a frequent aim for Breuer and Beckhard. Yet, among all of their houses, the so-called "Osprey Nest" on Fishers Island, New York, is perhaps the most sculptural; its very form is an abstract sculpture into which is fitted a wholly practical entity.

Ultimately, "Osprey Nest," named for the many nests of the endangered birds found on the small island, is a slightly deformed cube into which have been cut an entry, terraces, rooms, and windows. The only elements that affect the cube mass are a single chamfered corner and a subtle half-cylinder (looking not unlike an especially large engaged column) enclosing an interior stairway. Not only has the house been opened up on its sides, but also at the top or third floor where a significant amount of space is open to the sky with walls to encase the space.

Beckhard admits to an "abstract preoccupation with generating openings in a box" when designing the house. Yet, while the window placements and cutouts seem random, unpredictable, and deliberately abstract from the exterior, they make perfect sense from within.

The young couple who commissioned Beckhard did so after seeing an article about the Gagarin II House ("Big Sur") that Beckhard had designed in 1975. As the client recalls, he and his wife wanted a house that was "very simple, very pure, and that didn't have any affectations; we knew that was not a problem with [Beckhard] since he has a very pure view of structure."

Beckhard's first design was for a single-story house that both hugged and was set into the landscape (as with the "Big Sur" house), marked in part by a hillside. Shortly thereafter Beckhard and the Vasilious decided that a tall house would better take advantage of the views to the ocean and of the island terrain.

The living/dining area is divided, at least visually, by a bush-hammered concrete fireplace unit. A narrow diagonally cut pass-through notch lessens the solidity of the fireplace unit. Two exposed flues serve the living room fireplace and the dining room fireplace/grill, while the third flue provides fresh air to both as per energy requirements. In the background the low and high windows capture different views.

photo: © Andrew Appell 1984

The room on the third floor is used for everything from a study to a dance studio.
photo: © Andrew Appell 1984

The kitchen is tucked beneath the master bedroom while the dining room remains a part of the two-story-high main room.
photo: © Andrew Appell 1984

Beckhard developed a new plan.

The very height of the house was a daring feature on Fishers Island, an exclusive place within Long Island Sound noted for its strict design committees and stock of traditional two-story-high shingle-style houses. Fortunately, "Osprey Nest" passed all of the requirements, though the clients had to reassure the design committee that the third floor would not be used as a sleeping space. Other than the Koerfer house, no other Breuer/Beckhard house is as tall and multistoried.

The house's many windows, cutouts, and terraces make every facade active. The west facade, for instance, has the recessed entryway, the projecting circular stairway with a narrow window slit into it—not unlike what one would see in a medieval castle tower—a cutout on the third floor, and randomly alternating single- and double-pane windows. The main, or east,

elevation has a first floor wall of windows above which is a panel that acts as a sun screen, a balcony with cables as its railing, and a large cutout open to the sky on the third floor. So active are the facades with windows that looking from the outside it is a challenge to figure out where they might be situated in rooms. Some windows appear to fall mid-story while others seem to be flush with floors.

Here, as with many of the Breuer and Beckhard designs, the entrance is wholly recessed. It has an unexpected break with the geometry of the structure as it is placed at an angle.

The exterior cedar siding is stained with a clear gray hue to achieve a natural, weathered look. The client recalls Beckhard trying many shades of gray before finding the right one. Both he and Beckhard were adamant that the grain of the wood remain visible and that the color not seem arti-

ficial or opaque. As in several of his houses, Beckhard placed the wood vertically on the east and west facades and diagonally on the north and south to create a transition in both texture and appearance and to emphasize bracing qualities.

The contrast between moving from the protected, recessed entry into the house where one quickly sees the wall of windows capturing an ocean view is a dramatic one. Within this combined living/dining area the plan of the house is immediately revealed. Situated on two sides of this two-story-high space are bedrooms. From both the master bedroom and the hallway off the staircase that leads to two additional bedrooms, one can look down onto the space. A hinged panel can close off the master bedroom opening when increased privacy is desired. In an effort to keep the dining room distinct from the kitchen, an island counter unit separates the two spaces, though the kitchen is ultimately removed by its simply not being situated directly beneath the

On the north
and south sides
the cedar mem-
bers are placed
on the diagonal.
photo: © Andrew Appell
1984

two-story expanse.

The fireplace that distin-
guishes the living from the dining
area is monumental. Overtly sculptural and made of bush-hammered
concrete like many of the architects' fireplaces, this one is approximately six feet tall and rounded on both ends; while the fireplace opening on the living room
side is at a conventional height,
the opening on the dining side is
raised from the floor to allow for

cooking. The fireplace unit itself is
seemingly assembled in massive
pieces, each articulated by deep
grooves—a keen expression of
poured concrete technology. A
small pass-through element or
"window" cut at a diagonal lessens
the mass. Three flues, each within
bands of terra-cotta, rise up
through the house, emerging at the
third floor roof deck. Two flues,
each separated from an inner flue
liner by a layer of insulation, serve
the living room and dining room
side fireplaces, while the third
brings fresh air to both (a new energy code requirement). From the
outside on the east facade, the
reddish-brown flues are visible and
become an element of color in an
otherwise all-gray cedar house.
(The only other elements of color
are also visible on this facade; the
door to the ground floor terrace
and another directly above on the
balcony off the master bedroom
are trimmed in the ever-startling
Breuer-blue.)

A loft-like space on the third
floor, fitted with a mini kitchenette
and powder room, functions as a
dance studio for Mrs. Vasiliou, an
office, a television room, and an
observatory. The majority of the
third floor, however, is an open
deck, a facility that allows for outdoor dining and entertaining, and
sunbathing as it takes in views
from all directions. Walls with cutouts frame the space making it
feel more like a room than a terrace. Though made here in wood,
the cutouts are similar in configuration and feel to the earlier

Breuer/Beckhard stone cutout in
the courtyard of the Hooper house.
Two intersecting beams cross the
open deck where they act as
bracing members; tension wires
run from them to stabilize the
three flues. Though structural in
function, the beams nonetheless
capture outdoor space in a way
that the free-floating members do
so on the McMullen house.

It is important to realize that
Beckhard's solution was not simply
the result of deciding on a whim to
build a box and then fit rooms into
it. Clearly there was first an anal-
ysis of the program and then an
idea of how to arrange the rooms.
Ultimately, Beckhard discovered
that a single, strong form could
accommodate those needs and the
site. The Vasiliou house accomplishes what no other of the traditional houses on the island can:
capture every view. Furthermore,
outdoor living spaces have been
created within the very body of the
house, and seemingly unrelated
elevations with their parts situated
in unpredictable places on the
facade work to become a unified
composition.

The third floor deck
is an important
living space. Chim-
ney flues and brac-
ing beams articulate
the space, which
has views in three
directions.
photo: © Andrew Appell
1984

Recollections of Working with Marcel Breuer

Herbert Beckhard

First of all, Breuer was like a father to me. Exactly forty-two years ago, when I started working with him, he was fifty and I was twenty-five. Overall we had our good moments and bad, like any father and son situation, and I suppose that we had our disagreements (I probably had more with him than did the other young partners). Somehow I believe those disagreements brought us closer. I am told occasional difficulties tend to cement certain relationships. In retrospect I have nothing but the greatest affection for Lajko, as he was called. Not just affection, but unstinting admiration, respect, and appreciation for his teaching and sharing of experience and attitudes toward design. I am still very close to his wife, Connie, one of the finest persons I have known—wonderfully modest, considerate, and a true friend.

Of course, when we started out, Breuer was simply the architect and I was the draftsman. (He treated the situation on a more equitable basis and looking back it becomes apparent that I did manage to contribute on a higher level.) I was more than pleased with that role, "soaking up" all I could from the Master. The first project I worked on to a significant degree was a house in Princeton, New Jersey, for Marion Levy, a professor at the university. This occurred some few months after my start of employ. Breuer allowed me to do quite a lot on that project, including going out to the job for construction supervision as well as

preparing the design and technical documents. It was not long before he really threw me into the thick of things with the Gagarin house project where I became involved much more in dealings with the client as well as still being responsible for design, construction documents, and actual construction supervision.

The Gagarin house produced a very special experience for me since it was a very large and complex residential project. That extraordinary opportunity (considering my limited level of experience) featured dealing with Bobby Bigelow, a crusty and very knowledgeable carpenter/foreman who must rank as one of my very best "professors." It is noteworthy that after so short a period of time and my "callow youth," Breuer gave me the degree of responsibility that he did. In retrospect, I'm not sure why he did that unless he intuitively trusted me and thought I should handle it—sink or swim.

There certainly was no doubt at that time who was boss and who was working for whom, but with considerable speed (much greater than I could have anticipated) our professional relationship approached a close-to-even-status situation, although clearly Breuer was still always the number one man. Let's just say it shifted from a balance of 90/10 to 55/45 or some such ratio. Some five years from my first day at work I had been elevated to partner status along with my contemporaries, Hamilton Smith and Robert Gatje,

and our office manager, Murray Elmslie—an older, wiser hand. By then the office had expanded to a total staff of about thirty-five. Obviously, many clients, particularly house clients, were determined to deal with Breuer personally, but he was able to and seemed to want to (out of necessity—how much could one man do?) dilute that situation whenever possible. How to do that depended very much on the situation from client to client. Certainly after not too long we acted quite interchangeably, the aura and special power of the Breuer name notwithstanding. With larger projects, such as St. Francis de Sales Church in Muskegon, the Housing and Urban Development Headquarters Building, and the Health, Education, and Welfare Headquarters Building, a close-to-equal situation for the two of us was more easily achieved than with house clients.

Obviously we worked well as a team. We reached agreement on design and technical matters quite quickly and smoothly. The emphasis was on maintaining a high level of momentum and not overworking design to the point of staleness. My feeling is that Breuer was aware of the significant value of spontaneity and freshness to design and it is still my inclination to work in that manner. It is easy to complicate matters and be trapped by the multitude of design and technical solutions requiring resolution on all projects. Loss of momentum is, generally, disastrous. Relatively little seems to be

Marcel Breuer
photo: Hans Namuth

Herbert Beckhard, 1972
photo: Eleanor Beckhard

achieved by reworking and reconsidering matters time and time again. There is no stopping point in design and one could go on designing forever, but the degree of improvement on a project diminishes precipitously at a sometimes hard to recognize point.

Well, as Breuer got older and the firm got busier and larger an increasing degree of autonomy found its way to me as well as to the other now not quite so young partners, who now included Tician Papachristou and Mario Jossa, but no longer Murray Elmslie. That transition soon allowed people to state that they were easily aware of which partner was involved in a project prior to ever seeing the credits. Surely that was a sign of Breuer's increasing tendency to "loosen the reins" even while he was still healthy and strong.

After a significant number of productive years it all came to a halt. It was a sad day for me when Lajko took me to lunch and quietly handed me a letter indicating that his poor health forced him to re-

tire. He asked that I deliver the news to the other partners. He was truly a great person, very tough on his near-equals and very compassionate to all at the lower echelons. There was always the urge in the office to work with a staff of young people, perhaps with less experience but with more enthusiasm. They came from everywhere, representing the broadest international base. Lajko felt this produced a certain atmosphere. He was right and we still strive for diversity in our current office.

When I left the partnership about five years after Breuer's retirement and subsequent death in 1981, it was without rancor or disagreement. As partners we worked exclusively one-on-one with our mentor, to the exclusion of each other. For me the "raison d'être" for it all had expired.

Credit for any personal success which I have had must be acknowledged. My mother, who died very young, encouraged me as a young artist in my teens and earlier. My father, who must be categorized as an "amateur" architect, was a pillar of support with frequent minor design/construction assignments for me even during my student days. My ability to work for Breuer in 1951 as a volunteer (i.e., no pay) was in good part possible due to the unqualified understanding and support of my wife, Eleanor, a highly successful and well-paid model at the time. Her continued encouragement, and that of my fine

children, Susan, Karen, Tom, and Jane, has been key to my staying power in the difficult, often humbling, and mostly wonderful profession of architecture. And of course a special recognition goes to my partner of today, Frank Richlan, a key contributor and collaborator in my current work.

Herbert Beckhard, FAIA
May 1992

A Nostalgic Afterword

Stanley Abercrombie, FAIA
and editor in chief of *Interior Design*

My looking at the manuscript of David Masello's admirable book, like Proust's tasting his madeleine, has triggered a rush of half-forgotten personal memories, though I will try here to be a bit briefer than Proust.

In 1962 I arrived in New York to work for Marcel Breuer & Associates, and I stayed with the office three and a half years. During that happy time, I saw some of the houses in this collection being designed, worked on some of them myself, and studied the drawings of some of those already built.

The Breuer office was then at the northeast corner of Third Avenue and Fifty-seventh Street, above a Schrafft's restaurant—the particular taste associated with these memories therefore being not so much of madeleines as of egg-salad sandwiches. I was given a desk in a corner of the larger of two drafting rooms, which together probably held a maximum of two dozen. (The firm would later move to larger quarters.)

At the desk in front of mine was Richard Meier, who was extraordinarily kind and helpful to this young novice from Georgia, but who would soon leave to begin an independent career by designing a house for his parents. At the desk to my right was Herb Beckhard, an associate in the firm and my immediate boss, also kind and helpful but not, frankly, undemanding, either of his assistants or of himself. During my first months in the office, Herb, Richard, and I worked together on a large syna-

gogue of structurally adventurous folded concrete planes meant for a New Jersey suburb.

When the synagogue commission fell through (for reasons I no longer remember or perhaps never knew), I was put to work, under Herb, on a project much smaller but, I found, infinitely more interesting: an addition to Breuer's own modest summer cottage in Wellfleet, Massachusetts. It was a scale of work I found more appealing than that of the monumental temple; looking back, I think it may have been more congenial to Breuer and Herb as well.

In addition to Herb, Breuer's associates at the time were Hamilton Smith, Robert Gatje, and Murray Elmslie. Murray had the role of office manager; Herb, Ham, and Bob the role of project designers and managers. In the drafting room, we were an extraordinarily international stew; backgrounds were Russian, Chinese, Japanese, Danish, French-Moroccan, Italian, German, English, and Irish—the office joke being that I was admitted only because I represented the Confederacy.

Breuer himself was a constant presence, visiting the drafting boards daily. Although his decade of teaching at Harvard was then fifteen years behind him, he was very much the teacher still, and his board visits would never bring autocratic decisions but rather discussions of different possibilities and their likely con-

sequences; he was never too hurried to explain.

In the last of my years in the Breuer office, at my own request, I was moved from Herb's corner of the drafting room to the opposite corner so that I could work on the new commission for the Whitney Museum. This was a job headed by Ham Smith, but I kept in close touch with Herb by working, nights and weekends, doing the construction drawings for the house he was about to build for himself in Glen Cove. I well remember how much it mattered to Herb that the drawings not only be accurate and informative, but also beautifully composed and presented: each sheet, each detail, each note. Even after leaving the Breuer office, I continued to work occasionally for Herb on his residential projects, some of them additions to designs from the Breuer firm, some not; some included in this present selection, some not.

It seems to me that a young architect in the '60s could have had no better education than a few years in Breuer's drafting room, particularly if the assigned projects were largely residential, and most particularly if the projects were directed by Herb, who was entrusted with virtually all the office's house projects. Although all Breuer's associates (who later were made partners) had their own admirable strengths and talents, it was always my feeling that Herb's tastes, inclinations, and abilities were the closest to Breuer's own and that these found their clearest expression in works at the residential scale. In showing both the Breuer/Beckhard collaborations and the felicitous houses Herb has since designed on his own, this book, I think, confirms that feeling. In any case, it records some remarkable achievements that show, better than any other body of work I know, the humanity of Modern architecture at its best.

It also shows, when we look at the examples from the late '30s and '40s, the originality and vigor with which Breuer greeted his newly adopted America and its construction conventions. The austere forms and anonymous smooth surfaces of European modernism were left behind in the old country, replaced here with durable, low-maintenance, natural materials (most notably, wood frames, wood siding, and fieldstone) disposed in compositions that were becomingly modest and genuinely functional. These were not traditional houses in modern dress; they were genuinely new houses, thoughtfully planned to accommodate new patterns of living. Breuer invented a type of modern American house that in its way was both more modern and more American than any that existed before it.

It is a still valid house type if it is not practiced by rote but is reconsidered for each new combination of client, need, budget, and site. Such skillful reconsideration, such honest, investigative, inventively problem-solving design invigorates the powerful and appealing houses that Herb Beckhard con-

tinues to produce. Breuer would be proud of those houses, and of Herb.

Sketch by Stanley Abercrombie, Beckhard House, 1964

Color Plates

Beckhard House
living room
photo: Nick Wheeler

Breuer/Bratti House
west elevation
photo: Nick Wheeler

Breuer/Bratti guest
house and pool
photo: Nick Wheeler

Beckhard House
south elevation
photo: Andrew Appell

Breuer/Bratti House
living and dining area
photo: Nick Wheeler

Beckhard House
(left to right) dining
room, living room,
master bedroom
photo: Nick Wheeler

Cohen House
south view
photo: Gil Amiaga

Cohen House
west elevation
photo: Gil Amiaga

Gagarin I House
detail of west
elevation
photo: Otto Baitz

Koerfer House
view towards study
photo: Ben Schnall

Hooper House
west elevation
photo: Walter Smalling

Koerfer House
photo: Ben Schnall

Bornhorst House
south elevation
photo: Nick Wheeler

Koerfer House
interior staircase
photo: Ben Schnall

Hooper House
entry and courtyard
photo: Walter Smalling

Bornhorst House
east elevation
photo: Nick Wheeler

Breuer/Robeck House
living room
photo: Andrew Appell

Breuer/Robeck
House entry
photo: Andrew Appell

Breuer/Robeck
House
photo: Andrew Appell

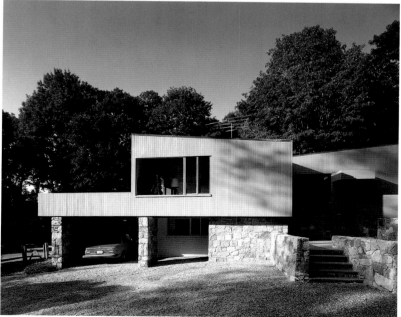

Geller II House
south elevation
photo: Tom Breuer

Schwartz House
view from west
photo: Andrew Appell

Schwartz House
south elevation
photo: Andrew Appell

Stillman II House
south elevation
photo: Otto Baitz

Schwartz House
master bedroom
photo: Andrew Appell

Schwartz House
kitchen
photo: Andrew Appell

Stillman II House
entry court
photo: Otto Baitz

Vasiliou House
photo: Andrew Appell

Vasiliou House
photo: Andrew Appell

Acknowledgments

More than anyone, I want to thank Herbert Beckhard for believing that I was the right one to write this book. Often interrupting a workday to spend time with me, Herb was also always willing to forfeit, or at least postpone, a tennis game (he is no mere amateur player) in order to meet with me, something I sensed he would not do with many people. I am grateful also to Stephen Kliment, editor in chief of *Architectural Record,* for recommending me in the first place for this project and for continuing to feed me assignments during it. Frank Richlan, Herb's partner, must also be thanked for letting me have such free rein in the office and with Herb. Marjorie Hoog, a senior associate in Herb's office, helped gather many of the photographs and track down other data. Ellie Beckhard, who among other things is a genuinely talented painter, is the kind of person you feel immediately comfortable with and close to, and her comments on the text were as important as anyone's. Alexander Schweder, a talented fourth-year student in the architecture program at Pratt Institute, proved to be a master at redrawing the plans that are used in the book; Gary Hansen, another promising architect in his final year at the New York Institute of Technology, and Shang-Peng Chen who makes the architectural models in Herb's office also worked on several of the plans. Herb's office assistants, Gail Worley and Stephanie Kramer, proved patient beyond measure in accommodating the countless meetings that I needed to have with Herb. My editor, Jim Mairs, was immediately receptive to my proposal for this book, and his decision to let me go ahead with it changed my entire professional agenda. Nancy Palmquist, W.W. Norton's managing editor, did an expert job in the copy editing. *Avenue* magazine's president, Judith Price, was supportive and generous in allowing me to maintain a very unorthodox schedule. My brother Robert, as always, was eager to offer much-needed advice, especially given the many books he has gone through; his wife, Laurie, also a writer, showed great support and interest. My brother Steve and his wife, Mary Joan, remained enthusiastic and inquiring–ingredients necessary to any writer. Susan Obrecht really did listen and remain interested in the project and encouraged me to be bolder than I otherwise would have been. Professor Bert Hornback at the University of Michigan was the one who helped me realize I could make a career out of writing about architecture. My Aunt Jo and Uncle Bob were great cheerleaders and were as interested in learning about the houses as I was. Special thanks to my great friend Donna Wilkinson whose support was always immediate and unqualified. And thanks of course to Tony Powell for his unwavering loyalty and affection. –DM

Index